The Very Pointless Quiz Book

Also by Alexander Armstrong and Richard Osman

The 100 Most Pointless Things in the World

The 100 Most Pointless Arguments in the World . . . Solved!

The Very Pointless Quiz Book

Alexander Armstrong and Richard Osman

First published in Great Britain in 2014 by Coronet
An imprint of Hodder & Stoughton
An Hachette UK company

First published in paperback in 2015

2

A CIP catalogue record for this title is available from the British Library

ISBN 978 1 444 78274 5
Ebook ISBN 978 1 444 78272 1

Typeset in Celeste by
Palimpsest Book Production Limited, Falkirk, Stirlingshire

Printed and bound by Clays Ltd, St Ives plc

Hodder & Stoughton policy is to use papers that are natural, renewable and recyclable products and made from wood grown in sustainable forests. The logging and manufacturing processes are expected to conform to the environmental regulations of the country of origin.

Hodder & Stoughton Ltd
Carmelite House
50 Victoria Embankment
London EC4Y 0DZ

www.hodder.co.uk

INTRODUCTION

Merry Christmas! Or, if you've waited for the paperback version of this book to come out, goodness it's hot isn't it?

This is our third *Pointless* book, and we think it's one of our very best. We'd go so far as to say it's definitely in the top three.

Our previous books involved us trying to write lots of jokes, and then sprinkling a few *Pointless* quizzes in between, but this year our publisher had a very interesting idea.

'Why not,' she suggested, 'have far more quizzes, and far fewer jokes from you two?' We were immediately interested in this idea. We burned all the jokes we had written (including a terrific one about a volcano in Peru) and collected 100 of our favourite *Pointless* questions instead.

That is the book you find before you: 100 questions of all shapes and sizes, to test every tuck and fold of your brain. It will be perfect to prove once and for all which member of your family is the cleverest, and which is the most effective cheat.

In between the quizzes we have also taken the liberty of answering every question we've ever been asked about

Pointless. So if you want any information at all about the *Pointless* trophy, Richard's computer, why Xander is so nice to everyone and which celebrities are awful cheats, it's all in here too.

So sit back, relax, pour yourself a drink, realize you have left this book on the sideboard, get up again with a loud 'tut', go over to the sideboard, pick up the book, go back to your seat, sit back, relax, pour yourself a drink and enjoy.

Gather the family around you, switch off the TV, suggest a nice friendly game of Pointless, hear the tinkling laughter of children, see the adults smiling and proudly ruffling the hair of their offspring, adjudicate over a disputed answer, try to break up the ensuing fight, drive your elderly uncle to A&E and weep over another Christmas ruined by the over-competitive gene that has cursed your family.

Our thanks once again this year to our invaluable *Pointless* gang. They really are the loveliest people in television. Particular thanks to the many members of the incredible *Pointless* questions team over the years. Their job is genuinely much harder than you would think, and they continue to do it with such creative brilliance year after year. Special mentions also to John Ryan, Molly Van Den Burgh and especially, for all his hard work, the wonderful Nick Shearing.

THE RULES

If you haven't played Pointless before, all you need to know is that every time you give an answer you have to try and think of the most obscure answer possible. Every single correct answer in Pointless has been tested in advance (we give one hundred people one hundred seconds to come up with as many answers as they can in order to work out our scores). You just have to scour the dark corners of your brain to find the answers the fewest of our one hundred people knew because the highest scoring team at the end of each round is eliminated. Good luck.

CAPITAL CITIES OF EUROPE

Any capital city of any country that is either wholly or partly in Europe. We will only accept answers that are the official capital city and the country must be a member of the United Nations in its own right.

POINTLESS FACT

This was the first question asked on the very first episode of *Pointless*.

AMSTERDAM	37	NICOSIA	2
ANDORRA LA VELLA	1	OSLO	39
ANKARA	1	PARIS	98
ATHENS	16	PODGORICA	0
BAKU	0	PRAGUE	27
BELGRADE	4	REYKJAVIK	4
BERLIN	62	RIGA	8
BERN	11	ROME	66
BRATISLAVA	4	SAN MARINO	0
BRUSSELS	42	SARAJEVO	0
BUCHAREST	4	SKOPJE	1
BUDAPEST	14	SOFIA	9
CHISINAU	0	STOCKHOLM	30
COPENHAGEN	36	TALLINN	7
DUBLIN	42	TBILISI	0
HELSINKI	16	THE HAGUE	10
KIEV	2	TIRANA	0
LISBON	40	VADUZ	2
LJUBLJANA	1	VALETTA	1
LONDON	93	VIENNA	14
LUXEMBOURG	0	VILNIUS	2
MADRID	65	WARSAW	16
MINSK	1	YEREVAN	0
MONACO	1	ZAGREB	3
MOSCOW	14		

POINTLESS FACT

The first answer given to this question was a pointless one (Podgorica), Xander had never heard of it (those heady days when we hadn't heard of remote European capitals, heavy elements on the Periodic Table, or tiny UN-recognized island nations in the South Pacific).

PEOPLE NAMED ALEX

We are going to show you twelve descriptions of famous people, male and female, past and present – each person is commonly known by a first name that could be shortened to 'Alex'. We would like you to tell us who they are please.

Author of 'The Beach'

Widely credited as the 'inventor' of the telephone

Beat JLS to win 'The X Factor' in 2008

Russian winner of 1970 Nobel Prize in Literature

Became leader of the Scottish National Party in 1990

18th-century poet who translated the works of Homer

ALEX GARLAND	7
ALEXANDER GRAHAM BELL	85
ALEXANDRA BURKE	29
ALEXANDER SOLZHENITSYN	18
ALEX SALMOND	37
ALEXANDER POPE	4

...Continued

PEOPLE NAMED ALEX

Frontman of the Arctic Monkeys

Scottish bacteriologist who discovered penicillin

Voice of Family Guy's 'Lois Griffin'

Married Katie Price in 2010

Author of 'The No.1 Ladies Detective Agency'

Became manager of Manchester United in 1986

ALEX TURNER	5
ALEXANDER FLEMING	40
ALEX BORSTEIN	0
ALEX REID	31
ALEXANDER MCCALL SMITH	7
ALEX FERGUSON	75

BRITISH LANDMARKS

We are going to show you five anagrams of famous landmarks from the UK. We would like you to identify the landmarks.

For landmarks that traditionally have a 'the' before their names, we have excluded the 'the' from the anagram.

HONEST GENE

LOONIES FAR UP THAMES

WORST CHIEF FIVEFOLD

UP RAMPANT CHOCOLATE

LECH SONS

STONEHENGE	**26**
HOUSES OF PARLIAMENT	**4**
WHITE CLIFFS OF DOVER	**2**
HAMPTON COURT PALACE	**0**
LOCH NESS	**30**

DAVID BOWIE UK TOP 40 STUDIO ALBUMS

Any studio album released by David Bowie as a solo artist, prior to the beginning of April 2011. Live albums and greatest hits compilations will not be accepted, and neither will albums he released as part of a group or collaboration.

ALADDIN SANE	6
BLACK TIE WHITE NOISE	0
DAVID BOWIE	4
DIAMOND DOGS	5
EARTHLING	0
HEATHEN	0
"HEROES"	9
'HOURS . . .'	0
HUNKY DORY	0
LET'S DANCE	6
LODGER	1
LOW	3
NEVER LET ME DOWN	1
OUTSIDE	1
PIN UPS	1
REALITY	1
RISE AND FALL OF ZIGGY STARDUST AND THE SPIDERS FROM MARS	18
SCARY MONSTERS (AND SUPER CREEPS)	0
SPACE ODDITY	7
STATION TO STATION	1
THE MAN WHO SOLD THE WORLD	3
TONIGHT	0
YOUNG AMERICANS	4

'We asked 100 people . . .'

Who are the 100 people you ask?

Nobody knows. They are carefully selected and polled online by a private polling company. All we know is that the information is checked and checked again and very closely guarded. People who get asked things like how they're going to vote in elections, which TV programmes they watch or how many nineteenth-century Foreign Secretaries they can name in a hundred seconds are either a) sworn to secrecy or b) very, very forgetful because in forty-four years on this good earth no-one has ever told me about it happening to them. Maybe it's done without them knowing? Maybe our pollsters have a number of barmen on their payroll and they only approach people when they're hammered? That, in fact, would explain rather a lot.

FAMOUS RICHARDS

We are going to show you a list of fourteen descriptions of people who are all known by the first name Richard. Please tell us who they are.

Author of 'The God Delusion'

Leading actor who appeared in 'Pretty Woman'

Comedian who co-starred in several films with Gene Wilder

German composer of 'Ride of the Valkyries' (1813–1883)

Actor who played Victor Meldrew

President of the United States (1969–1974)

Swaziland-born actor who starred in 'Withnail and I'

...Continued

FAMOUS RICHARDS

Actor who married Elizabeth Taylor twice

Businessman whose autobiography is 'Losing My Virginity'

Current 'Top Gear' TV presenter

Director and writer of 'Love Actually'

Former 'Blue Peter' and current Radio 5 Live presenter

Actor who starred in 'Close Encounters of The Third Kind'

TV presenter married to Judy Finnigan

RICHARD BURTON	77
RICHARD BRANSON	19
RICHARD HAMMOND	37
RICHARD CURTIS	8
RICHARD BACON	27
RICHARD DREYFUSS	21
RICHARD MADELEY	56

UNITS OF CURRENCY

In a moment, on the board, we are going to show you five units of currency. We are looking for the usual, short-form name in English of any country, other than the UK, that uses any of them as its main official unit of currency, as of February 2013.

By country, we mean a member of the United Nations that is a sovereign state in its own right.

We will not accept a country only because it has an overseas territory that uses any of these units of currency; e.g. we will not accept France just because French Polynesia uses the franc.

FRANC

PESO

POUND

RUPEE

SHILLING

FRANC	
BENIN	0
BURKINA FASO	0
BURUNDI	0
CAMEROON	0
CENTRAL AFRICAN REPUBLIC	0
CHAD	0
COMOROS	0
CONGO	0
CÔTE D'IVOIRE	0
DEMOCRATIC REPUBLIC OF CONGO	0
DJIBOUTI	0
EQUATORIAL GUINEA	0
GABON	0
GUINEA	0
GUINEA-BISSAU	0
LIECHTENSTEIN	0
MALI	0
NIGER	0
RWANDA	0
SENEGAL	0
SWITZERLAND	21
TOGO	0

PESO	
ARGENTINA	7
CHILE	2
COLOMBIA	1
CUBA	1
DOMINICAN REPUBLIC	0
MEXICO	45
PHILIPPINES	1
URUGUAY	0

POUND	
EGYPT	7
LEBANON	1
SOUTH SUDAN	0
SUDAN	0
SYRIA	0

RUPEE	
INDIA	90
MAURITIUS	1
NEPAL	1
PAKISTAN	3
SEYCHELLES	0
SRI LANKA	3

SHILLING	
KENYA	5
SOMALIA	1
TANZANIA	1
UGANDA	2

FIVE-WORD BOOK TITLES

Here is a list of books whose English-language title consists of five words. We have removed the second word from each title.

We want you to tell us which word completes the title please. The dates in brackets are the years in which the books were first published.

The _____ in the Willows (1908)

The _____ of Dorian Gray (1891)

The _____ and the Fury (1929)

The _____ in the Hat (1957)

The _____ of the Spirits (1982)

WIND	98
PICTURE	27
SOUND	7
CAT	75
HOUSE	4

SNOOKER PLAYERS WITH A MAXIMUM BREAK

Any snooker player who has recorded a maximum break in professional competition between 1982 and 2011, according to worldsnooker.com.

ADRIAN GUNNELL	0
ALAIN ROBIDOUX	0
ALI CARTER	1
ANDREW HIGGINSON	0
BARRY HAWKINS	0
BARRY PINCHES	0
CLIFF THORBURN	12
DAVID McDONNELL	0
DAVID McLELLAN	0
DING JUNHUI	2
GRAEME DOTT	2
JAMES WATTANA	0
JAMIE BURNETT	0
JAMIE COPE	0
JASON PRINCE	0
JIMMY WHITE	30
JOHN HIGGINS	9
JOHN PARROTT	7
JOHN REA	0
KARL BURROWS	0
KIRK STEVENS	7
KURT MAFLIN	0
LIANG WENBO	0
MARCO FU	2
MARCUS CAMPBELL	0
MARK SELBY	2
MEHMET HUSNU	0
NEIL ROBERTSON	0
NICK DYSON	0
PETER EBDON	2
ROBERT MILKINS	0
RONNIE O'SULLIVAN	32
RORY McLEOD	0
SHAUN MURPHY	0
STEPHEN HENDRY	21
STEPHEN MAGUIRE	0
STEVE DAVIS	67
STUART BINGHAM	1
THANAWAT THIRAPONGPAIBOON	0
TOM FORD	1
TONY DRAGO	1
TONY MEO	2
WILLIE THORNE	2

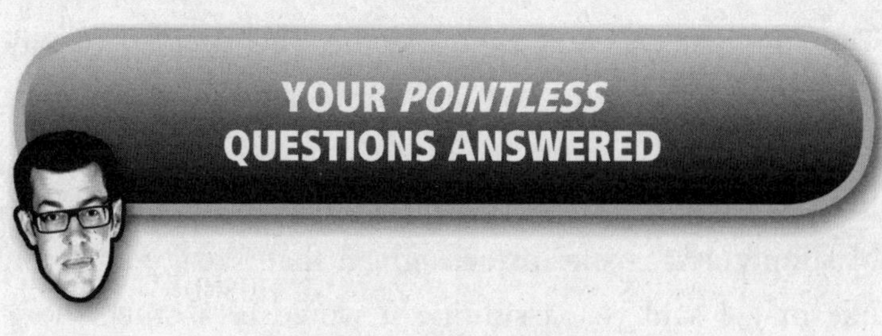

Who are you?

How on earth did you get to be on *Pointless*?

No offence taken.

I just mean I'd never seen you on anything before, and you don't seem like, well, a normal TV presenter. I thought maybe you'd been a comedian, but having watched for a while now that seems very unlikely.

Well my real job is a TV producer, and I've been doing that for over twenty years. Then I accidentally became a TV presenter.

Accidentally? How?

Well my company, Endemol, makes quiz shows, and about five years ago we came up with *Pointless* and tried to sell it to the BBC. To do that we invited them into a large hall and played a show for them. What we call a 'run-through'. For the run-through, as always, we played the role of the hosts ourselves. One of the creators of the show, Tom, played the main host, and I sat behind a desk playing the co-host. The run-through went well and the BBC decided to buy the show. About two days later Tom came up to my desk and said the BBC were trying to think of someone a bit like me to be the co-host, and they had hit upon the idea of simply asking me instead (given that I really am a bit like me). I said yes, assuming it would be a quiet, short-lived show on BBC2 and I could quickly get back to the peace and quiet of my day job.

But that didn't happen.

No, due to the wonderful format, the great producers and my lovely friend Xander the whole thing took off and I find that I have essentially turned into Bob Holness.

And have you given up the day job?

No, producing TV and thinking up new ideas is still my favourite thing in the world. But I'm very grateful that my life also took this unusual turn.

COUNTRIES WHICH HAVE WON THE EUROVISION SONG CONTEST

Can you name any country other than the UK that has won the Eurovision Song Contest at least once up to the end of 2011?

We are looking for the country name as it is commonly known in English. In the case of a former country that no longer exists, we want its name at the time of its victory.

AUSTRIA	1	MONACO	2
AZERBAIJAN	4	NETHERLANDS	6
BELGIUM	1	NORWAY	19
DENMARK	12	REPUBLIC OF IRELAND	71
ESTONIA	5	RUSSIA	12
FINLAND	18	SERBIA	4
FRANCE	42	SPAIN	27
GERMANY	39	SWEDEN	58
GREECE	19	SWITZERLAND	17
ISRAEL	34	TURKEY	9
ITALY	16	UKRAINE	5
LATVIA	5	YUGOSLAVIA	3
LUXEMBOURG	6		

PHILOSOPHERS AND THEIR FIRST NAMES

We're going to show you twelve famous philosophers, with their initials and dates of birth. We are looking for their usual first names as represented by these initials.

Where we give more than one initial we need the names represented by both initials.

N. CHOMSKY (1928)

T. AQUINAS (1225)

F. BACON (1561)

L. WITTGENSTEIN (1889)

B. RUSSELL (1872)

R. DESCARTES (1596)

NOAM 17

THOMAS 33

FRANCIS 62

LUDWIG 9

BERTRAND 29

RENÉ 26

...Continued

PHILOSOPHERS AND THEIR FIRST NAMES

J-P. SARTRE (1905)

B. PASCAL (1623)

F. NIETZSCHE (1844)

A. RAND (1905)

J. BENTHAM (1748)

K. MARX (1818)

JEAN-PAUL	48
BLAISE	12
FRIEDRICH	27
AYN	4
JEREMY	8
KARL	91

BURNS NIGHT SUPPER

We are going to show you some items of food or drink that all traditionally can feature in a Burns Night Supper, with alternate letters removed. We would like you to fill in the blanks for the food item you think the fewest of our 100 people knew.

C _ C _ A _ E _ K _ E   _ O _ P

T _ T _ I _ S

C _ L _ E _   S _ I _ K

T _ P _ Y   _ A _ R _

H _ G _ I _

COCK A LEEKIE SOUP	27
TATTIES	51
CULLEN SKINK	6
TIPSY LAIRD	1
HAGGIS	95

SITCOMS

RECURRING ACTORS IN 'GAVIN & STACEY'

Any actor or actress to have appeared in three or more episodes of the BBC sitcom 'Gavin and Stacey', according to the IMDB website, up to the start of March 2013.

RECURRING ACTORS IN 'MEN BEHAVING BADLY'

Any actor or actress to have appeared in three or more episodes of the UK sitcom 'Men Behaving Badly', according to the IMDB website, up to the start of March 2013.

We are including all episodes, regardless of the channel on which they were originally shown.

RECURRING ACTORS IN 'MRS BROWN'S BOYS'

We are looking for the name of any actor or actress to have appeared in three or more episodes of the BBC sitcom 'Mrs Brown's Boys', according to the IMDB website, up to the start of March 2013.

RECURRING ACTORS IN 'GAVIN & STACEY'

Actor	
ADRIAN SCARBOROUGH	0
ALISON STEADMAN	4
ANDREW KNOTT	0
DOMINIC GASKELL	0
EWAN KENNEDY	0
IFAN HUW DAFYDD	0
JAMES CORDEN	34
JASON GREGG	0
JOANNA PAGE	3
JOHNNY TUDOR	0
JULIA DAVIS	0
LARRY LAMB	7
MARGARET JOHN	0
MATHEW BAYNTON	0
MATHEW HORNE	5
MELANIE WALTERS	0
OSCAR HARTLAND	0
ROB BRYDON	7
ROBERT WILFORT	0
RUSSELL TOVEY	0
RUTH JONES	11
SAMUEL ANDERSON	0
SHERIDAN SMITH	0
STEFFAN RHODRI	0
STEVE MEO	0
WILLIAM THOMAS	0

RECURRING ACTORS IN 'MEN BEHAVING BADLY'

AMANDA DREW	0	LESLIE ASH	27
CAROLINE QUENTIN	26	MARTIN CLUNES	61
DAVE ATKINS	0	NEIL MORRISSEY	36
HARRY ENFIELD	3	ROBIN KERMODE	0
IAN LINDSAY	0	VALERIE MINIFIE	0
JOHN THOMSON	0	AMANDA WOODS	1

RECURRING ACTORS IN 'MRS BROWN'S BOYS'

BRENDAN O'CARROLL	8	GARY LILBURN	0
CONOR MOLONEY	0	JAMIE O'CARROLL	0
DANNY O'CARROLL	1	JENNIFER GIBNEY	0
DEREK REDDIN	0	MARK DYMOND	0
DERMOT O'NEILL	0	MARTIN DELANY	0
EILISH O'CARROLL	0	MIKE PYATT	0
EMILY REGAN	0	PADDY HOULIHAN	0
FIONA GIBNEY	0	PAT SHIELDS	0
FIONA O'CARROLL	0	RORY COWAN	0
GARY HOLLYWOOD	0	SMUG ROBERTS	0
		SUSIE BLAKE	1

YOUR *POINTLESS* QUESTIONS ANSWERED

Podiums

What's the best podium to be on?

The best podium is the last one because you have longer to think, giving you a better opportunity to get good ideas from other people's answers and to learn from their mistakes. The first podium frequently catches out the unwary. Many's the time a promising first pair have scored 100 with their first answer only for the rest of the round to be single-figure scores.

Then why don't people on the last podium always go through?

I'm not saying you're suddenly going to know all the answers on Podium Four, just that strategically you are the best placed to do well.

Unless of course all the quite-clever answers you knew on a board have gone and you're left with two stupidly obvious ones and one that's mad-genius-level obscure. Not so clever now is it?

Also, if you were planning say . . . a military assault on *Pointless,* on or around Podium Four would be the best place to set up a position.

What?

Because from there you've got a height advantage and optimal all-round visibility with clear simultaneous cover on the other three podiums, *and* Richard and me. Lob a whizz-bang into the tower, take the big man and me out of the game and Bob's your uncle, the operation is over almost before it's started.

Wow, that strayed quite far from the point.

I might just sit down for a minute if that's alright.

UK SPORTING CHAMPIONS AND THEIR SPORTS

We are going to show you fourteen men and women who were either born in, or have represented the UK and have been World Champions in their sport. Please tell us the sports in which each of these people have been world champion.

In each case, we want you to name the sport, and not the individual class or event.

PETER EBDON

DENNIS PRIESTLEY

BETH TWEDDLE

JOHN CONTEH

KAREN BRIGGS

NICK MATTHEW

JACKIE STEWART

SNOOKER	**39**
DARTS	**21**
GYMNASTICS	**47**
BOXING	**49**
JUDO	**5**
SQUASH	**4**
FORMULA 1	**85**

...Continued

UK SPORTING CHAMPIONS AND THEIR SPORTS

NORA PERRY

ALISTAIR BROWNLEE

JAMES CRACKNELL

LIAM TANCOCK

JAMES TOSELAND

BEN AINSLIE

VICTORIA PENDLETON

WORDS ENDING IN 'OO'

We are looking for any word that has its own entry in the 'Oxford Dictionary of English' ending with the letters 'oo'.

As usual we will not accept acronyms, proper nouns, trademarks, or hyphenated words. Nor will we accept any words marked as being 'offensive' by the dictionary.

ALOO	0	LOO	25
BALLYHOO	0	MOO	16
BAMBOO	2	MUNYEROO	0
BARCOO	0	NARDOO	0
BAZOO	0	NOONOO	0
BOO	17	PEEKABOO	0
BOOGALOO	0	POO	9
BOOHOO	0	POTOO	0
BROO	0	POTOROO	0
BUCKAROO	0	PUCKEROO	0
BUGABOO	0	RAZOO	0
BURGOO	0	ROO	1
CALLALOO	0	ROOKOO	0
COCKAPOO	0	SHAMPOO	3
COCKATOO	2	SHIVOO	0
COO	14	SHOO	5
CUCKOO	3	SKIDOO	0
DIDGERIDOO	0	SMACKEROO	0
FLOPPEROO	0	SWITCHEROO	0
GENTOO	0	TABOO	4
GOO	4	TATTOO	3
HALLOO	0	TOO	2
HOODOO	0	VINDALOO	1
HOOROO	0	VOODOO	1
HULLABALOO	3	WAHOO	0
IGLOO	17	WALLAROO	0
JACKAROO	0	WANDEROO	0
JILLAROO	0	WAZOO	0
KANGAROO	5	WOO	8
KAZOO	1	YAHOO	4
LADOO	0	ZOO	20

FAMOUS PEOPLE BORN IN THE UK

We are going to show you five anagrams of the names of famous people throughout history who were born in the UK. We've given their occupation in brackets. We would like you to give us their names.

BUSHY CROFTER (presenter)

BATTIER EXPORT (illustrator and writer)

NOW ACE SAINT (physicist)

SCRAWLIER HAND (naturalist)

I AM A WEAKISH SPELLER (playwright)

ADELE SONGS

We are looking for the title of any song on either of Adele's albums '19' or '21', or that has featured on a UK Top 40 single by Adele either as a title track or a B-side up to the end of 2012.

We are including tracks that appeared on deluxe or limited, or special digital editions of the albums.

However, we will accept a title only once, regardless of whether it was a studio, live or remix version of a song.

BEST FOR LAST	3	MANY SHADES OF BLACK	0
CHASING PAVEMENTS	15	MELT MY HEART TO STONE	2
COLD SHOULDER	3	MY SAME	1
CRAZY FOR YOU	1	NEED YOU NOW	0
DAYDREAMER	3	NOW AND THEN	0
DON'T YOU REMEMBER	0	ONE AND ONLY	5
FIRST LOVE	1	PAINTING PICTURES	0
FOOL THAT I AM	0	RIGHT AS RAIN	1
HE WON'T GO	1	ROLLING IN THE DEEP	24
HIDING MY HEART	0	RUMOUR HAS IT	6
HOMETOWN GLORY	4	SET FIRE TO THE RAIN	12
I CAN'T MAKE YOU LOVE ME	0	SKYFALL	27
I FOUND A BOY	0	SOMEONE LIKE YOU	21
IF IT HADN'T BEEN FOR LOVE	1	TAKE IT ALL	2
I'LL BE WAITING	3	THAT'S IT, I QUIT, I'M MOVIN' ON	1
LOVESONG	0	TIRED	3
MAKE YOU FEEL MY LOVE	4	TURNING TABLES	3

YOUR *POINTLESS* QUESTIONS ANSWERED

The computer

Hi Richard! What is on your computer?

Nothing.

How do you mean?

I mean nothing. It hasn't been plugged in for five years, and I've never looked at it.

So where do you get the questions from?

They're all on a piece of paper in front of me.

A piece of paper? Like in the olden days?

Exactly. The good thing about a piece of paper is that it never runs out of charge, it never gets hacked by Nigerian fraudsters, and it never tells you that you have to upgrade to 'piece of paper 6.1' with improved functionality and enhanced security options.

So why do you have a computer that doesn't work sitting on your desk?

Because this is television and an empty desk would look boring, and a pretend computer gives me an air of authority.

Like someone who works in a bank or something?

Yes, or like someone watching cat videos on YouTube when they're supposed to be working in a bank.

Television is ridiculous isn't it?

Yes it is. That's one of the many reasons that I love it.

ACTORS WHO HAVE PLAYED SUPERHEROES ON FILM

We are going to show you a list of four superheroes. We'd like you to name any actor who has been credited as playing any of these superheroes in a feature-length film up to August 2012. This excludes alter-egos, short films, TV films, TV programmes and voice performances. Straight-to-video and foreign-language films are also excluded.

BATMAN

HULK

SPIDERMAN

SUPERMAN

BATMAN

ADAM WEST	15
CHRISTIAN BALE	21
GEORGE CLOONEY	12
MICHAEL KEATON	28
VAL KILMER	17

HULK

EDWARD NORTON	4
ERIC BANA	3
MARK RUFFALO	2

SPIDERMAN

ANDREW GARFIELD	3
TOBEY MAGUIRE	13

SUPERMAN

BRANDON ROUTH	1
CHRISTOPHER REEVE	29
GEORGE REEVES	0

POINTLESS FACT

George Reeves starred in the 1951 film 'Superman and the Mole-Men' before going on to appear in the 'Adventures of Superman' TV series.

FAMOUS SHIPS

We will show you twelve descriptions of famous ships. We would like you to give us the names of these vessels.

WWII battleship named after Germany's 'Iron Chancellor'

Ship that took James Cook to Botany Bay

Armed vessel on which Fletcher Christian led a mutiny

Ship aboard which Nelson died at Trafalgar

Took Darwin to the Galapagos

Wreck of Henry VIII's warship raised in 1982

BISMARCK	**15**
HMS ENDEAVOUR	**2**
HMS BOUNTY	**22**
HMS VICTORY	**26**
HMS BEAGLE	**8**
MARY ROSE	**38**

...Continued

FAMOUS SHIPS

US battleship, scene of Japan's surrender in WWII

Ship in which Sir Francis Drake made his voyage of circumnavigation (1577–1580)

Took the first Pilgrim Fathers to New England

British Royal yacht retired in 1997

Subject of an influential 1925 Soviet silent film

Tea clipper preserved at Greenwich

USS MISSOURI 3

GOLDEN HIND 9

THE MAYFLOWER 19

HMY BRITANNIA 29

POTEMKIN 6

CUTTY SARK 28

SHAKESPEARE'S COMEDIES

We are going to show you five sets of numbers that relate to the number of letters in the usual short titles of comedies written by Shakespeare, like you get at the end of crossword clues.

We'd like you to give us the title of the play represented by the numbers.

2,3,4,2

4,3,5,7

3,5,5,2,7

1,9,6,5

4,4,4,4,4

AS YOU LIKE IT	34
MUCH ADO ABOUT NOTHING	30
THE MERRY WIVES OF WINDSOR	11
A MIDSUMMER NIGHT'S DREAM	66
ALL'S WELL THAT ENDS WELL	7

UK MPS CALLED DAVID, NICK, OR ED

Quite simply we are looking for any male UK Member of Parliament as of May 2012, who is listed on the parliament.uk website as having first name of 'David', 'Nick', or 'Ed'. Or variants thereof, i.e. 'Dave', 'Nicholas', 'Edward', etc.

We would like you to name the one you think is the most obscure.

DAVE WATTS	0	DAVID SIMPSON	1
DAVID AMESS	1	DAVID TREDINNICK	0
DAVID ANDERSON	1	DAVID WARD	0
DAVID BLUNKETT	5	DAVID WILLETTS	0
DAVID BURROWES	0	DAVID WINNICK	0
DAVID CAMERON	97	DAVID WRIGHT	0
DAVID CRAUSBY	0	ED BALLS	61
DAVID DAVIES	3	ED MILIBAND	74
DAVID DAVIS	4	EDWARD DAVEY	1
DAVID EVENNETT	0	EDWARD GARNIER	0
DAVID GAUKE	0	EDWARD LEIGH	0
DAVID HAMILTON	0	EDWARD TIMPSON	0
DAVID HANSON	0	EDWARD VAIZEY	0
DAVID HEATH	0	NIC DAKIN	0
DAVID HEYES	0	NICHOLAS SOAMES	2
DAVID JONES	0	NICK BOLES	1
DAVID LAMMY	0	NICK BROWN	0
DAVID LAWS	1	NICK CLEGG	90
DAVID LIDINGTON	0	NICK DE BOIS	0
DAVID MILIBAND	49	NICK GIBB	0
DAVID MORRIS	0	NICK HARVEY	0
DAVID MOWAT	0	NICK HERBERT	1
DAVID MUNDELL	0	NICK HURD	0
DAVID NUTTALL	0	NICK RAYNSFORD	1
DAVID RUFFLEY	0	NICK SMITH	0
DAVID RUTLEY	0		

POINTLESS FACT

This was the question where a contestant infamously made up a name, 'Nick Brown', and it turned out to be a correct, and pointless, answer.

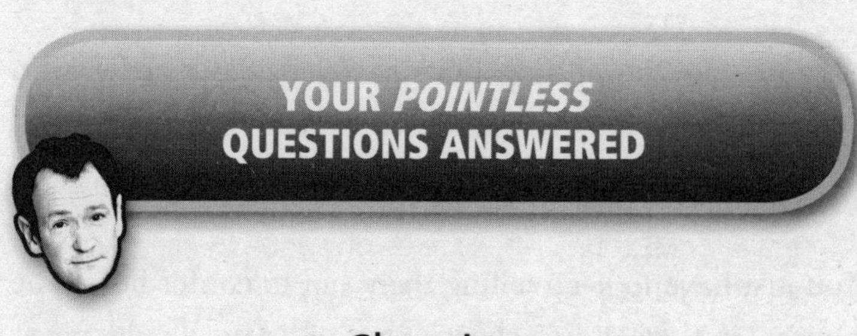

Cheating

Has anyone ever cheated?

The only way you could possibly cheat on *Pointless* would be by whispering answers to your team-mate, and as every contestant has a microphone, we can hear even the tiniest noise they make so, so far, that has never happened. Just as well, as it would be embarrassing. There is an episode of Lee Mack's excellent *Not Going Out* where Lee comes on *Pointless* and does cheat by sneaking into Richard's dressing-room before the show and looking at the questions. This actually wouldn't work in real life because Richard doesn't see the questions until the show starts. Also he has two female ex-Mossad bodyguards on full-time duty.

Are you saying the celebrities never cheat?

No, I am not saying that. When celebrities come on the show they all cheat like mad.

Why?

Because they never stop talking. Celebs can't come on a show and stand quietly unless they've been specially trained.

What can you do?

You just have to keep telling them not to confer but, to be honest, if they didn't cheat some of them would never know the answers . . .

Who have been your favourite celebrities?

We've had amazing people on since we started the celebrity shows – everyone from Mary Berry to Sir Geoff Hurst, Todd Carty to Josh Widdicombe. We're always so touched when people agree to come on because it's not an easy show to do – there's always a chance something will come up that you don't know at all – and yet they keep coming.

MR MEN CHARACTERS WITH A 'Y' IN THEIR NAME

We're looking for the names of any Mr Men characters, published in English as part of the Mr Men series written by Roger Hargreaves, that have a letter 'Y' in their name.

We are including the books written by Roger Hargreaves and co-written by his son Adam, as long as they have Roger Hargreaves' name credited as the author on the front. This is up to the start of 2013.

We will not accept the names of any characters created for limited edition or charity books.

MR BIRTHDAY	1
MR BUSY	6
MR CLUMSY	8
MR DAYDREAM	2
MR DIZZY	8
MR FUNNY	17
MR FUSSY	7
MR GREEDY	14
MR GRUMPY	40
MR HAPPY	70
MR JELLY	7
MR LAZY	12
MR MESSY	16
MR NOBODY	3
MR NOISY	6
MR NOSEY	13
MR SILLY	17
MR SKINNY	5
MR TOPSY-TURVY	7
MR UPPITY	8
MR WORRY	3

WINES AND THEIR REGIONS

The following are all wines or wine regions. We want to know the name of the countries with which they are most closely associated.

CHAMPAGNE

STELLENBOSCH

DAO VALLEY

CHIANTI

HUNTER VALLEY

RETSINA

FRANCE	84
SOUTH AFRICA	9
PORTUGAL	4
ITALY	62
AUSTRALIA	17
GREECE	32

...Continued

WINES AND THEIR REGIONS

SANCERRE

BAROLO

LIEBFRAUMILCH

MENDOZA

TOKAJI

RIOJA

FRANCE	36
ITALY	15
GERMANY	80
ARGENTINA	5
HUNGARY	7
SPAIN	46

OPEN GOLF CHAMPIONS

We are going to show you five anagrams of men who have won the Open Golf Championship since 1970. We'd like you to tell us who they are.

RANK DECLARER

WRITES GOOD

PICNICKER

SWAN MOTTO

FIND A LOCK

DARREN CLARKE	0
TIGER WOODS	43
NICK PRICE	6
TOM WATSON	12
NICK FALDO	15

BRITISH BATS

We are looking for any bat species found in the wild in the UK. To clarify, we are looking for resident species according to the Bat Conservation Trust – (their definition of 'resident' is that it breeds here). We will only accept the common English names, not the Latin names.

ALCATHOE BAT	6
BARBASTELLE	5
BECHSTEIN'S BAT	1
BRANDT'S BAT	4
BROWN LONG-EARED BAT	4
COMMON PIPISTRELLE	1
DAUBENTON'S BAT	0
GREATER HORSESHOE BAT	0
GREY LONG-EARED BAT	0
LEISLER'S BAT	0
LESSER HORSESHOE BAT	0
NATHUSIUS' PIPISTRELLE	0
NATTERER'S BAT	0
NOCTULE	0
SEROTINE	1
SOPRANO PIPISTRELLE	0
WHISKERED BAT	1

YOUR *POINTLESS* QUESTIONS ANSWERED

Tall

Hey Richard!

Hey you! Are you enjoying the quizzes?

Totes! And you were right, it is SO easy to cheat. Now, can I ask you a personal question?

Is the question 'how tall are you'?

Yes.

Ok, go on then.

Thanks. How tall are you?

I'm 6'7".

Wow.

I know, right?

And what size shoes do you take?

Wow again. And hat size?

I don't know. But probably an extra-large.

FAMOUS SCOTS

We are going to show you descriptions of fourteen famous Scottish people. We have given you the initials of the names by which they are most commonly known. We would like you to tell us their full names.

Pop singer and star of BBC documentary series 'The Big Time' (SE)

Philosopher who wrote 'Dialogues Concerning Natural Religion' (DH)

Inventor who was a principal developer of the steam engine (JW)

Celebrity chef, restaurateur and TV personality (GR)

Sang 'I Dreamed a Dream' on 'Britain's Got Talent' (SB)

Record-breaking athlete and inspiration for 'Chariots of Fire' feature film (EL)

Leader of Scottish independence, defeated the army of Edward I (WW)

SHEENA EASTON 16

DAVID HUME 3

JAMES WATT 35

GORDON RAMSAY 36

SUSAN BOYLE 64

ERIC LIDDELL 8

WILLIAM WALLACE 47

...Continued

FAMOUS SCOTS

Three-time Formula 1 World Drivers' Champion (JS)

Usually credited as the discoverer of penicillin (AF)

Host of TV series 'Changing Rooms' from 1996 to 2003 (CS)

Businesswoman and founder of a Glasgow-based lingerie brand (MM)

Co-presenter on breakfast-time TV show 'Daybreak' (LK)

Former Liverpool FC player and manager (KD)

Lead singer of rock group Travis (FH)

JACKIE STEWART	45
ALEXANDER FLEMING	29
CAROL SMILLIE	25
MICHELLE MONE	7
LORRAINE KELLY	46
KENNY DALGLISH	63
FRAN HEALY	16

US STATES THAT ARE SMALLER THAN ENGLAND

We are looking for any of the twenty-two US states that are smaller than England in terms of total land area.

We are only counting land area, so are not including water areas a state may possess including inland, coastal, Great Lakes, and territorial waters.

To give you an idea, the smallest state that is larger than the total land area of England is Alabama, so we're essentially looking for any US state smaller than Alabama. We will not accept Washington DC (also known as the District of Columbia) as it's not a US state.

CONNECTICUT	15
DELAWARE	9
HAWAII	30
INDIANA	3
KENTUCKY	7
LOUISIANA	5
MAINE	18
MARYLAND	11
MASSACHUSETTS	13
MISSISSIPPI	3
NEW HAMPSHIRE	9
NEW JERSEY	15
NEW YORK	28
NORTH CAROLINA	8
OHIO	18
PENNSYLVANIA	3
RHODE ISLAND	15
SOUTH CAROLINA	9
TENNESSEE	5
VERMONT	11
VIRGINIA	8
WEST VIRGINIA	7

WHALES

We are going to show you the names of five species of marine animals that can all be classed either as toothed or baleen whales. However, we have removed alternate letters from their names.

We would like you to tell us the name of the species you think the fewest of our 100 people knew.

B _ W _ E _ D

N _ R _ H _ L

H _ M _ B _ C _

M _ N _ E

B _ L _ G _

BOWHEAD 10

NARWHAL 37

HUMPBACK 82

MINKE 38

BELUGA 51

SPORT IN 2013

ANDY MURRAY'S WIMBLEDON VICTORY

We would like the name of any opponent Murray defeated in the Men's Singles at Wimbledon in 2013 en route to winning the title. We require first and second names.

BRITISH & IRISH LIONS 2013

We would like the name of any player who made an appearance for the British & Irish Lions in any of the three tests against Australia in the 2013 tour. We will accept players who made appearances as permanent replacements but not those who were unused substitutes. We will require first names and surnames.

PREMIER LEAGUE GOALSCORERS 2012/2013

We would like the name of any player who scored ten or more goals during the 2012/2013 Premier League season. We are only counting goals scored in the league – not in other competitions. We require first names and surnames or the name by which the player is commonly known.

ANDY MURRAY'S WIMBLEDON VICTORY

BENJAMIN BECKER	0
FERNANDO VERDASCO	1
JERZY JANOWICZ	1
MIKHAIL YOUZHNY	0
NOVAK DJOKOVIC	25
TOMMY ROBREDO	0
YEN-HSUN LU	0

BRITISH & IRISH LIONS 2013

ADAM JONES	0
ALEX CORBISIERO	0
ALEX CUTHBERT	0
ALUN WYN JONES	1
BEN YOUNGS	0
BRIAN O'DRISCOLL	4
CONOR MURRAY	0
DAN COLE	0
DAN LYDIATE	0
GEOFF PARLING	0
GEORGE NORTH	1
JAMIE HEASLIP	0
JAMIE ROBERTS	0
JONATHAN DAVIES	0
JONATHAN SEXTON	0
JUSTIN TIPURIC	0
LEIGH HALFPENNY	4
MAKO VUNIPOLA	0
MANU TUILAGI	0
MIKE PHILLIPS	1
OWEN FARRELL	0
PAUL O'CONNELL	0
RICHARD HIBBARD	0
RICHIE GRAY	0

SAM WARBURTON 7
SEAN O'BRIEN 0
TOBY FALETAU 0
TOM CROFT 0
TOM YOUNGS 0
TOMMY BOWE 0

PREMIER LEAGUE GOALSCORERS 2012/2013

ADAM LE FONDRE 0
AROUNA KONÉ 0
CARLOS TÉVEZ 0
CHRISTIAN BENTEKE 0
DANIEL STURRIDGE 2
DEMBA BA 0
DIMITAR BERBATOV 0
EDIN DŽEKO 1
FRANK LAMPARD 9
GARETH BALE 2
JAVIER HERNÁNDEZ 0
JERMAIN DEFOE 0
JUAN MATA 2
KEVIN NOLAN 0
LUIS SUÁREZ 17
LUKAS PODOLSKI 0
MAROUANE FELLAINI 0
MICHU 0
OLIVIER GIROUD 1
RICKIE LAMBERT 1
ROBIN VAN PERSIE 24
ROMELU LUKAKU 0
SANTI CAZORLA 0
SERGIO AGÜERO 8
STEVEN FLETCHER 0
THEO WALCOTT 2

YOUR *POINTLESS* QUESTIONS ANSWERED

Keeping cheerful

Do you never get bored of the show?

Genuinely never. Partly because the questions are always clever and challenging, partly because the contestants are always different and amusing in their own way, but mainly because of the cocktail of weapons-grade hallucinogens that Richard and I take for our own amusement.

What's the worst thing that can happen during a recording?

A computer failure. It sometimes starts with something small like one of the screens not working, or a sparkly little pixel flashing half-way up the tower. And we stop while Colin, who's very much in charge of sparkly pixels, comes and takes a look. If Colin can't fix it several other people come and take a look. If they start fiddling with something that's a long way from where the sparkly pixel is you know it might be something serious.

What happens if it's something serious?

First they'll re-boot the system, then they'll put it through the spare computer and if that doesn't work, we all go home.

Has that ever happened?

Only once in nearly 800 episodes. The other thing that happens is a contestant sometimes gives an answer that is borderline right so we have to stop while a debate rages 'upstairs' over whether we give it to them or not.

Where do you and Richard stand on those arguments?

We always want to give the benefit of the doubt, but then you've got to be fair to contestants in the past who had their answers harshly marked.

Sounds like a minefield.

Exactly my friend – we've discovered that the only way you can do it fairly is to be harsh to everyone.

SPORTING TERMS

We are going to show you some terms which are associated with particular sports – there are two terms for each sport.

We would like you to tell us the sport most commonly associated with these terms. By 'sport' we mean a general name rather than a particular variant. For example, we'd be looking for 'Athletics' rather than 'Sprinting' or 'Decathlon'.

By 'sporting term' for the purpose of this question, we mean a word which is used to refer to the equipment, strategies, positions or rules of a particular sport.

CHAIN GANG/NICKEL DEFENCE

HAIRPIN NET SHOT/TUMBLE DROP SHOT

HOME PLATE/INFIELD FLY

HIKE OUT/SPINNAKER

POINTS IN THE PAINT/PUMP FAKE

CLEAN AND JERK/SNATCH

CLINCH/QUEENSBERRY RULES

AMERICAN FOOTBALL 11

BADMINTON 4

BASEBALL 50

SAILING 23

BASKETBALL 7

WEIGHTLIFTING 40

BOXING 41

...Continued

SPORTING TERMS

CARROM BALL/ GARDENING

PELOTON/DROPPING WHEELS

STROKE JUDGE/PULLBUOY

RIP ENTRY/TUCK

ANKLE TAP/SCRUMMAGING

COCK FEATHER/FLETCHING JIG

POT/ PUSH STROKE

CRICKET	7
CYCLING	28
SWIMMING	3
DIVING	28
RUGBY UNION	61
ARCHERY	15
SNOOKER	44

FICTIONAL BEARS

The correct answers here are all fictional bears featured in books, comics, films and television. And all the incorrect answers are not fictional bears at all.

FOZZIE

YOGI

BALOO

COLUMBUS

SUPERTED

RUPERT

SHARDIK

FOZZIE	3
YOGI	63
BALOO	16
COLUMBUS	X
SUPERTED	2
RUPERT	49
SHARDIK	0

...Continued

FICTIONAL BEARS

PADDINGTON

FARGAS

BUNGLE

BARNABY

IOREK BYRNISON

SOOTY

BOO BOO

PADDINGTON	70
FARGAS	X
BUNGLE	1
BARNABY	0
IOREK BYRNISON	0
SOOTY	7
BOO BOO	19

STUDIO ALBUMS BY THE BEATLES

We will show you five sets of initials that represent titles of some studio albums released by The Beatles. We would like you to tell us what the initials stand for.

R

BFS

MMT

WTB

SPLHCB

REVOLVER 49

BEATLES FOR SALE 7

MAGICAL MYSTERY TOUR 18

WITH THE BEATLES 11

SGT PEPPER'S LONELY HEARTS CLUB BAND 63

CLASSIC SLAPSTICK COMEDIES

LAUREL & HARDY FEATURE FILMS

We are looking for the title of any feature film for which both Stan Laurel and Oliver Hardy received an acting credit. We will not accept short films, foreign-language versions of their American films, films in which they make uncredited cameo appearances or anthology or compilation films.

BUSTER KEATON FEATURE FILMS

We are looking for the title of any feature film for which Buster Keaton received an acting credit, according to IMDB. We will not accept short films, foreign-language versions of his American films, films in which he makes uncredited cameo appearances or anthology or compilation films.

FEATURE FILMS DIRECTED BY CHARLIE CHAPLIN

We are looking for the title of any feature film for which Charlie Chaplin received a directing credit, according to IMDB. We will not accept short films, anthology or compilation films. We will not accept 'Shoulder Arms', which, although listed by IMDB, is, at forty-five mins, arguably a short film.

LAUREL & HARDY FEATURE FILMS

Film	
A CHUMP AT OXFORD	0
A-HAUNTING WE WILL GO	0
AIR RAID WARDENS	1
ATOLL K	1
BABES IN TOYLAND	0
BLOCK-HEADS	0
BONNIE SCOTLAND	0
GREAT GUNS	0
HOLLYWOOD PARTY	0
JITTERBUGS	0
NOTHING BUT TROUBLE	0
OUR RELATIONS	0
PACK UP YOUR TROUBLES	0
PARDON US	4
PICK A STAR	0
SAPS AT SEA	0
SONS OF THE DESERT	4
SWISS MISS	0
THE BIG NOISE	0
THE BOHEMIAN GIRL	0
THE BULLFIGHTERS	0
THE DANCING MASTERS	0
THE DEVIL'S BROTHER	0
THE FLYING DEUCES	1
THE ROGUE SONG	0
WAY OUT WEST	5

BUSTER KEATON FEATURE FILMS

Film	Count
A FUNNY THING HAPPENED ON THE WAY TO THE FORUM	0
AROUND THE WORLD IN 80 DAYS	0
BATTLING BUTLER	0
BEACH BLANKET BINGO	0
COLLEGE	0
DOUGHBOYS	0
DUE MARINES E UN GENERALE	0
EL COLMILLO DE BUDA	0
EL MODERNO BARBA AZUL	0
FOREVER AND A DAY	0
FREE AND EASY	0
GO WEST	0
GOD'S COUNTRY	0
HOLLYWOOD CAVALCADE	0
HOW TO STUFF A WILD BIKINI	0
IN THE GOOD OLD SUMMERTIME	0
IT'S A MAD, MAD, MAD, MAD WORLD	0
LE ROI DES CHAMPS-ÉLYSÉES	0
LIMELIGHT	0
L'INCANTEVOLE NEMICA	0
OUR HOSPITALITY	0
PAJAMA PART	0
PARLOR, BEDROOM AND BATH	0
SAN DIEGO, I LOVE YOU	0
SERGEANT DEADHEAD	0
SEVEN CHANCES	0
SHERLOCK, JR.	0
SIDEWALKS OF NEW YORK	0
SPEAK EASILY	0
SPITE MARRIAGE	0
STEAMBOAT BILL, JR.	0
SUNSET BOULEVARD	0
THAT NIGHT WITH YOU	0
THAT'S THE SPIRIT	0
THE ADVENTURES OF HUCKLEBERRY FINN	0
THE CAMERAMAN	0
THE GENERAL	11
THE INVADER	0
THE LOVABLE CHEAT	0
THE MARCH OF TIME	0
THE MISADVENTURES OF BUSTER KEATON	0
THE NAVIGATOR	0
THE PASSIONATE PLUMBER	0
THE SAPHEAD	0
THE VILLAIN STILL PURSUED HER	0
THREE AGES	0
TROUBLE CHASER	0
WHAT – NO BEER?	0
YOU'RE MY EVERYTHING	0

FEATURE FILMS DIRECTED BY CHARLIE CHAPLIN

Film	
A COUNTESS FROM HONG KONG	2
A KING IN NEW YORK	1
A WOMAN OF PARIS: A DRAMA OF FATE	0
CITY LIGHTS	0
LIMELIGHT	2
MODERN TIMES	4
MONSIEUR VERDOUX	0
THE CIRCUS	0
THE GOLD RUSH	6
THE GREAT DICTATOR	13
THE KID	7

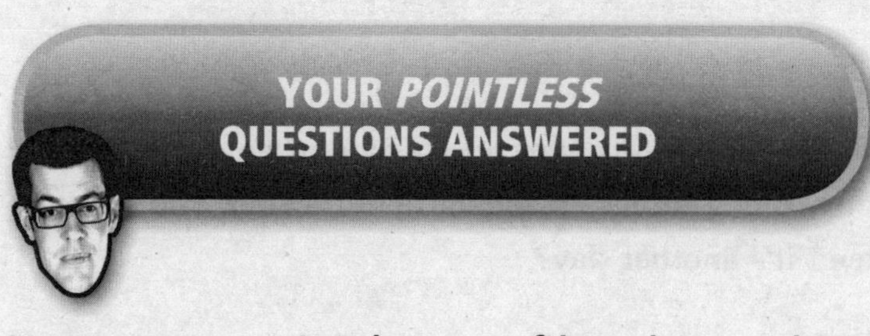

How many episodes are filmed in a day?

How many episodes do you film in a day?

Usually four.

Why so many?

It's all about cost. The most expensive part of making a TV show is the studio and all the people needed to make a studio work.

Like camera people and lighting people?

Exactly, and Producers and Directors, and people making tea for Producers and Directors, and counsellors to look after the people who have to make tea for Producers and Directors.

So the more shows in one day the better?

Exactly. If you're paying a flat rate for a studio for the day then it makes sense to film four episodes instead of one. Four times cheaper.

Then why don't you make five a day?

Please don't suggest that; we're already quite sleepy.

So do contestants film an episode, change clothes and then film another episode straight away? And you pretend it's another day?

Yep.

Television is ridiculous isn't it?

I think we've covered this already.

EUROPEAN FOOTBALL LEAGUE CHAMPIONS

We are about to show you the names of six top-flight football leagues in Europe (along with the nation in brackets). We'd like you to tell us the name of a football team that has won one of those leagues from the 1999/2000 season, through to the 2010/2011 season please.

BUNDESLIGA (Germany)

EREDIVISIE (Netherlands)

LA LIGA (Spain)

LIGUE 1 (France)

SCOTTISH PREMIER LEAGUE (UK)

SERIE A (Italy)

BUNDESLIGA (GERMANY)

Bayern Munich	26
Borussia Dortmund	7
VfB Stuttgart	0
VfL Wolfsburg	3
Werder Bremen	2

EREDIVISIE (NETHERLANDS)

AFC Ajax	14
AZ Alkmaar	3
FC Twente	4
PSV Eindhoven	8

LA LIGA (SPAIN)

Deportivo de La Coruna	0
FC Barcelona	42
Real Madrid	39
Valencia CF	2

LIGUE 1 (FRANCE)

AS Monaco FC	2
FC Nantes	0
Girondins de Bordeaux	0
Lille Olympique Sporting Club	4
Olympique de Marseille	5
Olympique Lyonnais	10

SCOTTISH PREMIER LEAGUE (UK)

Celtic	42
Rangers	41

SERIE A (ITALY)

AC Milan	21
AS Roma	4
Internazionale/Inter Milan	14
Juventus FC	10
SS Lazio	2

LITERARY VILLIANS AND THEIR WORKS OF FICTION

In which novel or play do these villains feature?

MRS DANVERS

BIG BROTHER

MISS TRUNCHBULL

BILL SIKES

GEORGE WICKHAM

MILADY DE WINTER

REBECCA	10
NINETEEN EIGHTY-FOUR	36
MATILDA	53
OLIVER TWIST	31
PRIDE AND PREJUDICE	12
THE THREE MUSKETEERS	6

...Continued

LITERARY VILLIANS AND THEIR WORKS OF FICTION

LONG JOHN SILVER

IAGO

SHERE KHAN

URIAH HEEP

MR KURTZ

MRS COULTER

TREASURE ISLAND	55
OTHELLO	10
THE JUNGLE BOOK	49
DAVID COPPERFIELD	3
HEART OF DARKNESS	1
NORTHERN LIGHTS (HIS DARK MATERIALS)	14

NINETEENTH-CENTURY PRIME MINISTERS

Here are the names of five people who were all Prime Minister of the UK at some point during the nineteenth century. We have taken out alternate letters of their names. We would like you to fill in the blanks and name them please. The names shown do not include any titles, such as Lord or Sir.

R _ B _ R _ P _ E _

S _ E _ C _ R P _ R _ E _ A _

J _ H _ R _ S _ E _ L

W _ L _ I _ M G _ A _ S _ O _ E

B _ N _ A _ I _ D _ S _ A _ L _

ROBERT PEEL	45
SPENCER PERCEVAL	4
JOHN RUSSELL	30
WILLIAM GLADSTONE	39
BENJAMIN DISRAELI	34

MANIC STREET PREACHERS UK TOP 40 SINGLES

We're looking for the title of any UK Top 40 single released by the Welsh band the Manic Street Preachers prior to the start of October 2012.

Double A-sides will be counted as separate answers. Collaborations do count as long as the band were a named, credited artist. We will only accept the titles as according to the Official Charts company.

We won't allow EPs, such as 'Life Becoming a Landslide'.

(IT'S NOT WAR) JUST THE END OF LOVE 0
A DESIGN FOR LIFE 11
AUSTRALIA 5
AUTUMNSONG 1
EMPTY SOULS 1
EVERYTHING MUST GO 5
FASTER 2
FOUND THAT SOUL 1
FROM DESPAIR TO WHERE 1
IF YOU TOLERATE THIS YOUR CHILDREN WILL BE NEXT 11
INDIAN SUMMER 1
KEVIN CARTER 3
LA TRISTESSE DURERA (SCREAM TO A SIGH) 3
LET ROBESON SING 1
LITTLE BABY NOTHING 1
LOVE'S SWEET EXILE 2
MOTORCYCLE EMPTINESS 9
OCEAN SPRAY 1
PCP 1
REPEAT 0
REVOL 1
ROSES IN THE HOSPITAL 0
SHE IS SUFFERING 0
SLASH 'N' BURN 4
SO WHY SO SAD 0
STAY BEAUTIFUL 3
THE EVERLASTING 3
THE LOVE OF RICHARD NIXON 0
THE MASSES AGAINST THE CLASSES 4
THEME FROM M.A.S.H. (SUICIDE IS PAINLESS) 3
THERE BY THE GRACE OF GOD 0
TSUNAMI 5
YOU LOVE US 5
YOU STOLE THE SUN FROM MY HEART 2
YOUR LOVE ALONE IS NOT ENOUGH 1

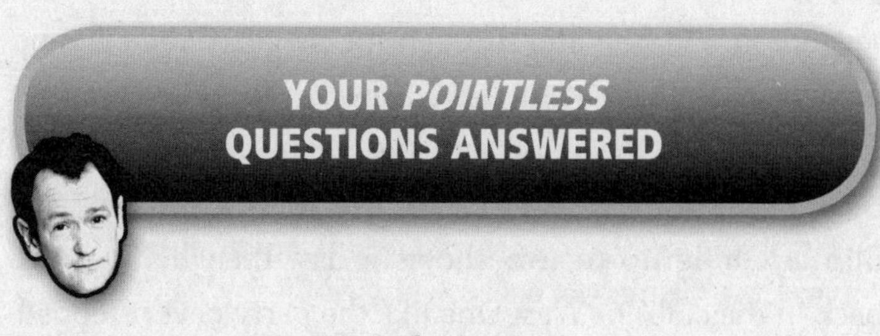

Drunkenness

Have you ever recorded an episode of *Pointless* drunk?

I'm struggling to think of when we've done one sober. Richard and I usually get to the studio at about 10am, arriving in an open-top sports car full to the brim with booze and young female cast members from *Emmerdale*. Then we hit Elstree, and it's like the circus has come to town. Proper carnage. John, our producer, says sometimes he can only find us by the trail of empty Jim Beam bottles and sequins. Somehow he gets us into the make-up chair for 11.30 with a little help from Dr Mojito and a few judiciously chosen restoratives from his medicine cabinet. Come midday though it's time to be professional. With an early-evening ITV lovely on each arm and a Moët in each fist we stride like heroes onto the studio floor. A quick swig of black coffee while make-up remove the last of the streamers from our hair and boom! The Pointless express has left the station.

We laugh a lot on that stage, occasionally we fight and,

yes, we cry a bit too. Each show takes between five and seven hours to film and through the magic of the edit and modern sampling techniques a coherent forty-five minutes is drawn from the noise and the flailing of two men in their professional prime. When the going's good we can film anything up to two shows a day, then by 11 we're back in the clubs of West One like the party never stopped. Next day it starts all over again – only thing that changes is the girls.

FAMOUS BASS PLAYERS

We are about to show you a list of 14 bass players. We would like you to tell us the name of the band of which they were members, with which they had their greatest chart success.

STING

JOHN DEACON

GUY BERRYMAN

GENE SIMMONS

DOUGIE POYNTER

ADAM CLAYTON

MIKE DIRNT

THE POLICE	53
QUEEN	12
COLDPLAY	4
KISS	28
McFLY	13
U2	18
GREEN DAY	3

...Continued

FAMOUS BASS PLAYERS

GEDDY LEE

PAUL McCARTNEY

JOHN PAUL JONES

ROGER WATERS

JOHN ENTWISTLE

CHRISTOPHER WOLSTENHOLME

FLEA

RUSH	6
THE BEATLES	80
LED ZEPPELIN	9
PINK FLOYD	22
THE WHO	25
MUSE	1
RED HOT CHILI PEPPERS	12

BIRDS IN THE UK

Here are six words. We are looking for the common name of any bird that includes one of these words and appears on the British Ornithologists Union's 'British List' for 2012 – this is the official list of all bird species recorded in Britain.

To be clear, your answer should include one of the following six words and only birds that appear on the BOU's 2012 British List will count.

BUNTING

FINCH

GROUSE

OWL

THRUSH

TIT

BUNTING

Black-faced Bunting	0
Black-headed Bunting	0
Chestnut-eared Bunting	0
Cirl Bunting	1
Corn Bunting	5
Cretzschmar's Bunting	0
Indigo Bunting	0
Lapland Bunting	1
Little Bunting	0
Ortolan Bunting	0
Pallas's Reed Bunting	0
Pine Bunting	0
Reed Bunting	7
Rock Bunting	0
Rustic Bunting	0
Snow Bunting	2
Yellow-breasted Bunting	0
Yellow-broned Bunting	0

FINCH

Bullfinch	2
Chaffinch	33
Citril Finch	0
Goldfinch	22
Greenfinch	19
Hawfinch	3
Scarlet Rosefinch	0
Trumpeter Finch	0

GROUSE

Black Grouse	5
Red Grouse	7

OWL

Barn Owl	72
Hawk Owl	0
Little Owl	10
Long-eared Owl	7
Scops Owl	1
Short-eared Owl	4
Snowy Owl	18
Tawny Owl	52
Tengmalm's Owl	0

THRUSH

Black-throated Thrush	0
Blue Rock Thrush	0
Dusky Thrush	0
Eyebrowed Thrush	0
Grey-cheeked Thrush	0
Hermit Thrush	0
Mistle Thrush	17
Naumann's Thrush	0
Northern Waterthrush	0
Red-throated Thrush	0
Rock Thrush	0
Siberian Thrush	0
Song Thrush	32
Swainson's Thrush	0
Thrush Nightingale	0
Varied Thrush	0
White's Thrush	0
Wood Thrush	1

TIT

Bearded Tit	1
Blue Tit	90
Coal Tit	21
Crested Tit	1
Great Tit	40
Long-tailed Tit	8
Marsh Tit	2
Penduline Tit	0
Willow Tit	2

FOOTBALLING RIVALRIES

We will show you five sets of initials of pairs of football teams, known for their great rivalries – along with the name of the matches between the two teams.

The initials stand for the common short-name of the team, with generic initials such as FC, AS, etc., removed.

We would like you to name both teams.

E v L (Merseyside derby)

KC v OP (The Soweto derby)

A v F (De Klassieker)

C v R (Old Firm)

B v RM (El Clásico)

FAMOUS PARENTS AND THEIR CHILDREN

OZZY OSBOURNE OR KELLY OSBOURNE

We are looking for the title of any single by either Ozzy Osbourne or Kelly Osbourne, or both, that has reached the Top 40 in the UK charts, as of the end of February 2013.

To clarify, we are looking for any single for which at least one of them received a solo credit or was a featured artist. This does not include anything by Black Sabbath – they must have been credited as artists in their own right. Double-A sides will count as two individual answers.

KINGSLEY AMIS OR MARTIN AMIS

We are looking for any published novels written by either Kingsley Amis or Martin Amis.

We will accept novels written under a pseudonym, or with a co-author.

VANESSA REDGRAVE OR JOELY RICHARDSON

We are looking for the title of any feature film for which either Vanessa Redgrave or Joely Richardson or both has received an acting credit, up to the end of February 2013, according to the IMDB website. This excludes any short films or films only ever shown on TV, but does include voice work.

OZZY AND KELLY OSBOURNE SINGLES

BARK AT THE MOON	3
CHANGES	23
DREAMER	1
GETS ME THROUGH	0
NO MORE TEARS	2
ONE WORD	0
PAPA DON'T PREACH	4
PERRY MASON	0
SHOT IN THE DARK	1
SHUT UP	1
SO TIRED	0

KINGSLEY AND MARTIN AMIS NOVELS

COLONEL SUN	0
DEAD BABIES	2
DIFFICULTIES WITH GIRLS	0
ENDING UP	0
GIRL, 20	0
HOUSE OF MEETINGS	0
I LIKE IT HERE	0
I WANT IT NOW	0
JAKE'S THING	0
LIONEL ASBO	0
LONDON FIELDS	3
LUCKY JIM	10
MONEY	8
NIGHT TRAIN	0
ONE FAT ENGLISHMAN	0
OTHER PEOPLE	0
RUSSIAN HIDE-AND-SEEK	0
STANLEY AND THE WOMEN	0

SUCCESS	0	THE GREEN MAN	0
TAKE A GIRL LIKE YOU	0	THE INFORMATION	0
THAT UNCERTAIN FEELING	0	THE OLD DEVILS	1
THE ALTERATION	0	THE PREGNANT WIDOW	1
THE ANTI-DEATH LEAGUE	0	THE RACHEL PAPERS	1
THE BIOGRAPHER'S MOUSTACHE	0	THE RIVERSIDE VILLAS MURDER	0
THE CRIME OF THE CENTURY	0	THE RUSSIAN GIRL	0
THE EGYPTOLOGISTS	0	TIME'S ARROW	4
THE FOLKS THAT LIVE ON THE HILL	0	WE ARE ALL GUILTY	0
		YELLOW DOG	0
		YOU CAN'T DO BOTH	1

VANESSA REDGRAVE AND JOELY RICHARDSON FILMS

Film	
101 Dalmatians	8
A Man for All Seasons	1
A Month by the Lake	0
A Proposito di Quella Strana Ragazza	0
A Rumour of Angels	0
A Wall of Silence	0
Agatha	0
Animals United	0
Anonymous	1
Atonement	1
Bear Island	0
Behind the Mask	0
Blow-Up	1
Body Contact	0
Camelot	2
Cars 2	0
Comrades	0
Consuming Passions	0
Coriolanus	0
Cradle Will Rock	0
Crime and Punishment	0
Deep Impact	2
Déjà Vu	0
Diceria Dell'Untore	0
Dropout	0
Drowning by Numbers	0
Evening	0
Event Horizon	0
Girl, Interrupted	0
Good Boy!	0
Gud, Lukt Och Henne	0
Hollow Reed	0
How About You . . .	0
Howards End	2
I'll Do Anything	0
Isadora	1
Julia	1
King Ralph	0
La Vacanza	0
Letters to Juliet	1
Little Odessa	
Loch Ness	0
Lulu on the Bridge	0
Mary, Queen of Scots	0
Maybe Baby	2
Miral	0
Mirka	0
Mission: Impossible	2
Morgan: A Suitable Case for Treatment	0
Mother's Boys	0
Mrs Dalloway	0
Murder on the Orient Express	0
Oh! What a Lovely War	0
Out of Season	0
Pokhorony Stalina	0
Prick Up Your Ears	0
Rebecca's Daughters	0
Red Lights	0
Restraint	0
Return to Me	0
Romeo & Juliet	0
Shining Through	0
Shoreditch	0
Short Order	0
Sing Sing	0
Sister My Sister	0
Smilla's Feeling for Snow	0
Song for Marion	1
Sparrow	
Steaming	0
Thanks for Sharing	0
The Affair of the Necklace	0
The Ballad of the Sad Café	0
The Bostonians	0
The Charge of the Light Brigade	0
The Christmas Miracle of Jonathan Toomey	0
The Devils	1
The Fever	0
The Girl with the Dragon Tattoo	2
The Hotel New Hampshire	0
The House of the Spirits	0
The Keeper	0
The Last Mimzy	0
The Last Will and Testament of Rosalind Leigh	0
The Patriot	1
The Pledge	0
The Riddle	0
The Sailor from Gibraltar	0
The Sea Gull	0
The Seven-per-Cent Solution	0
The Thief Lord	0
The Three Kings	0
The Tribe	0
The Trojan Woman	0
The Whistleblower	0
The White Countess	0
Un Tranquillo Posto di Campagna	0
Under Heaven	0
Uninvited	0
Venus	0
Wagner	0
Wetherby	2
Wilde	0
Wrestling with Alligators	0
Yanks	0

YOUR *POINTLESS* QUESTIONS ANSWERED

How can I be on the show?

Can I be a contestant on *Pointless*?

Not by yourself, no.

Ok, can me and my dad be contestants on *Pointless*?

You'll have to apply I'm afraid. And are you sure your dad is the best bet? You know what he's like.

Alright, say me and my mum, or my newsagent, or anyone except my dad wanted to apply. How would we do it?

When applications are open you'll find the details at www.bbc.co.uk/beonashow.

And what happens after we apply?

If the contestant team (who are all lovely, talented and terrifically good looking) enjoy your application form you'll be spoken to on the phone and then the lucky few will be invited to auditions up and down the country.

And what do you look for in contestants?

A real mix, but the greatest quality of all is to be a very nice person who people will enjoy watching.

I definitely won't ask my dad then.

And if you make it past the audition you'll be joining us on the show. Actually hanging out with me and Xander and discovering the many secrets that only *Pointless* contestants will ever know.

Oooh, like what?

Like the code for the contestants toilet.

What are my chances of getting on the show, and using that very toilet?

Well we have thousands of applications every series, but if you're bright and interesting your chances are high. And if you're bright and interesting and you've baked us a cake, then you're in.

NATIONS THAT HAVE PLAYED ENGLAND AT A RUGBY UNION WORLD CUP FINALS TOURNAMENT

We are looking for the name of any national rugby union team that has played against England in an IRB Rugby World Cup Finals tournament, since the inaugural tournament in 1987 up to the last tournament played to date, in 2011.

ARGENTINA	18
AUSTRALIA	60
FIJI	15
FRANCE	56
GEORGIA	1
ITALY	25
JAPAN	4
NEW ZEALAND	65
ROMANIA	3
SAMOA	11
SCOTLAND	37
SOUTH AFRICA	45
TONGA	8
UNITED STATES	6
URUGUAY	0
WALES	49

GERMAN BODY PARTS

We are going to show you the names of twelve body parts in German. We'd like you to tell us their English translations.

DAS AUGE

DER KOPF

DAS KNIE

DER NAGEL

DAS OHR

DIE ZUNGE

EYE	14
HEAD	37
KNEE	60
NAIL	9
EAR	22
TONGUE	10

...Continued

GERMAN BODY PARTS

DIE NASE

DER ZEH

DAS KINN

DER ELLENBOGEN

DER MAGEN

DER FINGERKNÖCHEL

NOSE 86

TOE 4

CHIN 12

ELBOW 32

STOMACH 3

KNUCKLE 34

FILM TITLES WITH BOYS' NAMES

Here are five films and the dates they were released. The missing word in each case is a boy's name. Please supply the missing words.

COOL HAND ____ (1967)

____'S ROOM (1996)

____ SCISSORHANDS (1990)

____ CLAYTON (2007)

I AM ____ (2001)

LUKE	78
MARVIN	5
EDWARD	95
MICHAEL	15
SAM	11

SHIPS OF THE ROYAL NAVY

We are looking for the name of any commissioned vessel that is listed as part of the fleet on the Royal Navy's website.

This is as of November 2012 and includes ships and submarines serving in the fleet.

We will not accept HMS Victory, which is listed as the flagship of the Second Sea Lord. We will also not accept decommissioned vessels, any new vessels that have not yet been commissioned such as HMS Ambush, or ships that are part of the Royal Fleet Auxiliary.

HMS Albion	7
HMS Archer	0
HMS Argyll	0
HMS Astute	0
HMS Atherstone	0
HMS Bangor	0
HMS Biter	0
HMS Blazer	0
HMS Blyth	0
HMS Brocklesby	0
HMS Bulwark	4
HMS Cattistock	0
HMS Charger	0
HMS Chiddingfold	0
HMS Clyde	0
HMS Daring	3
HMS Dasher	0
HMS Dauntless	4
HMS Defender	1
HMS Diamond	2
HMS Dragon	1
HMS Duncan	0
HMS Echo	0
HMS Edinburgh	3
HMS Endurance	1
HMS Enterprise	2
HMS Example	0
HMS Exploit	0
HMS Explorer	0
HMS Express	0
HMS Grimsby	0
HMS Hurworth	0
HMS Illustrious	7
HMS Iron Duke	0
HMS Kent	0
HMS Lancaster	0
HMS Ledbury	0
HMS Mersey	0
HMS Middleton	0
HMS Monmouth	0
HMS Montrose	0
HMS Northumberland	1
HMS Ocean	4
HMS Pembroke	0
HMS Penzance	0
HMS Portland	0
HMS Protector	0
HMS Puncher	0
HMS Pursuer	0
HMS Quorn	0
HMS Raider	0
HMS Ramsey	0
HMS Ranger	0
HMS Richmond	0
HMS Sabre	0
HMS Scimitar	0
HMS Scott	0
HMS Severn	0
HMS Shoreham	0
HMS Smiter	0
HMS Somerset	0
HMS St Albans	0
HMS Sutherland	0
HMS Talent	0
HMS Tireless	0
HMS Torbay	0
HMS Tracker	0
HMS Trenchant	0
HMS Triumph	0
HMS Trumpeter	0
HMS Tyne	0
HMS Vanguard	1
HMS Vengeance	1
HMS Victorious	2
HHMS Vigilant	0
HMS Westminster	0
HMSML Gleaner	0

POINTLESS FACT

The last question asked on the final episode of *Pointless* recorded at TC6 at Television Centre in what was the last TV programme to be made there.

YOUR *POINTLESS* QUESTIONS ANSWERED

Prize money

Why is the prize money so low?

Well, it's not *that* low. The least you can win is a half-share of £1,000, and five hundred quid is quite a tidy sum to have in your back pocket. Think how happy you'd be if you won that on the Grand National – it would be the best day ever.

Yes, but it's not a million is it?

Yes and that's brilliant because it's not going to ruin your life. You don't have to go off and buy a massive house or a silly car or anything like that, there'll be no-one turning up and demanding their share of the spoils, it's not going to make you want to go into work and swear at your boss, or feel you have to live out your days in the tropics drinking too much and moaning about how you miss *EastEnders* and Marmite. What it will pay for though is a brilliant night out with your family or a lovely weekend away. Or a puppy.

Puppy? Hmm I hadn't thought about a puppy.

See?

SISTER ACTS

We are looking for any act which is either a group or duo that features the word 'sister' or 'sisters' and has had a UK Top 40 hit up to the start of May 2012.

BEVERLEY SISTERS	28
DE CASTRO SISTERS	0
HANNAH & HER SISTERS	0
KAYE SISTERS	2
MCGUIRE SISTERS	0
SCISSOR SISTERS	48
SHAKESPEARS SISTER	17
SISTER 2 SISTER	0
SISTER SLEDGE	43
SUPERSISTER	0
SWING OUT SISTER	8
THE DALE SISTERS	0
THE ENGLAND SISTERS	0
THE POINTER SISTERS	20
THE SHEPHERD SISTERS	0
THE SISTERS OF MERCY	10
THE SURPRISE SISTERS	0
TWISTED SISTER	10

ISLANDS OF THE WORLD

Here is a list of clues to well-known islands around the world. We would like you to tell us the name of the island described by each clue please.

In the case of islands which are part of a country, we are looking for the name of the island itself, rather than the name of the country, although some of the islands may be countries in their own right

The largest and southernmost of the Channel Islands

One of the Galapagos Islands, which was the original home of Lonesome George

Canadian island which gave its name to a breed of working dog

Island which was awarded the George Cross in 1942

Australian island state, discovered by a Dutch explorer in 1642

French island, birthplace of Napoleon Bonaparte

JERSEY	41
PINTA	1
NEWFOUNDLAND	9
MALTA	22
TASMANIA	28
CORSICA	18

...Continued

ISLANDS OF THE WORLD

The largest of Ireland's 'Aran Islands'

Island which is divided between Indonesia, Malaysia and Brunei

Largest island in the Mediterranean located at the tip of Italy

Large island country near Africa to which many species of lemur are indigenous

One of the world's largest islands, part of the Kingdom of Denmark

English name for the island of 'Rapa Nui', famed for its giant stone statues

INISHMORE	**0**
BORNEO	**3**
SICILY	**35**
MADAGASCAR	**21**
GREENLAND	**13**
EASTER ISLAND	**28**

NURSERY RHYME CHARACTERS

Here are five anagrams of well-known nursery rhyme characters. We'd like you to name the characters.

FLEET LIFTS SUMMIT

MOODY LONG RUNS

JOLT THICK LEARNER

COCO BRINK

PUMP DUTY MYTH

LITTLE MISS MUFFET	14
SOLOMON GRUNDY	0
LITTLE JACK HORNER	24
COCK ROBIN	1
HUMPTY DUMPTY	68

LONDON 2012

OPENING CEREMONY – THE SEVEN 'BRITISH OLYMPIC HEROES'

Any of the seven 'British Olympic Heroes' who famously passed the Olympic torch to a young British athlete during the opening ceremony.

TEAM GB OLYMPIANS WHO WON GOLD ON 'SUPER SATURDAY'

Any of the twelve members of Team GB who won a Gold Medal on Saturday 4th August 2012 – commonly known as 'Super Saturday', when GB won gold in six events in a single day.

SPORTS IN WHICH TEAM GB WON ONE OR MORE PARALYMPIC MEDALS

Any Paralympic SPORT in which Team GB won at least one medal (of any colour) at the 2012 Paralympic Games in London.

To clarify, we are only looking for the name of the SPORTS listed on the London 2012 website – we are not looking for the names of individual events within those sports.

OPENING CEREMONY – THE SEVEN 'BRITISH OLYMPIC HEROES'

DALEY THOMPSON	13	MARY PETERS	3
DUNCAN GOODHEW	1	SHIRLEY ROBERTSON	0
KELLY HOLMES	12	STEVE REDGRAVE	31
LYNN DAVIES	1		

TEAM GB OLYMPIANS WHO WON GOLD ON 'SUPER SATURDAY'

ALEX GREGORY	0	KATHERINE COPELAND	0
ANDREW TRIGGS HODGE	0	LAURA TROTT	0
DANI KING	0	MO FARAH	51
GREG RUTHERFORD	9	PETE REED	0
JESSICA ENNIS	39	SOPHIE HOSKING	0
JOANNA ROWSELL	0	TOM JAMES	0

SPORTS IN WHICH TEAM GB WON ONE OR MORE PARALYMPIC MEDALS

Sport	Medals	Sport	Medals
ARCHERY	6	ROWING	7
ATHLETICS	21	SAILING	1
BOCCIA	0	SHOOTING	1
CYCLING	29	SWIMMING	58
EQUESTRIAN	15	TABLE TENNIS	0
JUDO	2	WHEELCHAIR TENNIS	2
POWERLIFTING	0		

YOUR *POINTLESS* QUESTIONS ANSWERED

Questions

Do you write all the questions yourself?

No, we have an amazing team of six people who spend their entire year coming up with Pointless questions.

Six of them? Surely it's pretty easy to write a couple of questions?

Well, let me describe to you how you get a single question onto the show. Firstly find a list that we haven't used on the show before. This is virtually impossible, because we've already used about 3000 lists. Then research every single answer, then verify every single answer via three independent sources (Wikipedia does not count as an independent source). Then send your list to the online polling organization and see how our 100 people perform. Then throw your list away because the 100 either knew way too much or way too little, so the question is unusable. In the rare event that it is usable, then research facts for every single possible answer, and finally pitch the question to the Series

Producer and hope she's in a good mood. And then repeat this process day after day after day.

Wow.

I know.

They must be superheroes!

They are. Bronagh has super-strength, Julia can teleport, Nick is almost always invisible and Rose has lasers for eyes.

And I bet they're a good pub quiz team?

I have come up against them a few times and they are unbeatable.

Do they ever get anything wrong?

No. People always tweet me to say we've got questions wrong, but that's always because they haven't listened to the question or criteria properly, or they've just looked at Wikipedia and Wikipedia has got it wrong. Occasionally I get stuff wrong, but that's always the stuff I come up with myself, and is entirely my fault.

Could I be one of your question team?

It is a cool job, but if you're very clever, very creative and immensely hard working then it could be for you. If you think all you have to do is say 'We should do a round on Harry Potter!' then it might not be.

NATURALLY OCCURING OBJECTS AND PHENOMENA IN SPACE

The correct answers in this round are all naturally occurring objects, systems and phenomena in space.

NEBULA

STAR

QUASAR

CORELLIA

ASTEROID

BOLIDE

WHITE DWARF

POINTLESS FACT

The first question in the first broadcast episode of *Pointless Celebrities* – on 4th July 2011.

NEBULA	7
STAR	70
QUASAR	2
CORELLIA	X
ASTEROID	38
BOLIDE	0
WHITE DWARF	4

...Continued

NATURALLY OCCURING OBJECTS AND PHENOMENA IN SPACE

COMET

PULSAR

SUPERNOVA

PROTOSTAR

ZANATTA

PLANET

GALAXY

COMET	39
PULSAR	3
SUPERNOVA	6
PROTOSTAR	0
ZANATTA	X
PLANET	62
GALAXY	27

POINTLESS FACT

It was probably around about this same time back in 2011 that someone on Twitter first made the joke, 'Wow, they really are pointless celebrities', that remains popular to this day.

FICTIONAL ADDRESSES

Here are twelve addresses from film, TV and literature, along with the initials of one of their residents. We'd like you simply to tell us the name of the character who resides there from the initials provided.

62 West Wallaby Street, Wigan, Lancs (G.)

124 Conch Street, Bikini Bottom, Pacific Ocean (S.S.)

4 Privet Drive, Little Whinging, Surrey (H.P.)

13 Coronation Street, Weatherfield, Greater Manchester, UK (H.O.)

Danemead, St Mary Mead (J.M.)

7 Eccles Street, Dublin, Ireland (L.B.)

GROMIT 7

SPONGEBOB SQUAREPANTS 20

HARRY POTTER 36

HILDA OGDEN 26

JANE MARPLE 7

LEOPOLD BLOOM 1

...Continued

FICTIONAL ADDRESSES

Apartment 1901, Elliott Bay Towers, Seattle, Washington (F.C.)

742 Evergreen Terrace, Springfield, USA (H.S.)

32 Windsor Gardens, Notting Hill, London (P.B.)

Pemberley, Derbyshire, UK (F.D.)

221B Baker Street, London, UK (S.H.)

1630 Revello Drive, Sunnydale, California (B.S.)

FRASIER CRANE	7
HOMER SIMPSON	46
PADDINGTON BEAR	6
FITZWILLIAM DARCY	0
SHERLOCK HOLMES	92
BUFFY SUMMERS	5

SURNAMES OF PRESIDENTS THAT END IN 'N'

We are looking for the surnames of any US Presidents which end in the letter 'n', prior to Barack Obama. Where more than one President shared the same surname, that surname will only be accepted once.

BUCHANAN	1
CLINTON	47
HARRISON	1
JACKSON	5
JEFFERSON	15
JOHNSON	18
LINCOLN	48
MADISON	1
NIXON	75
REAGAN	33
TRUMAN	10
VAN BUREN	0
WASHINGTON	30
WILSON	7

YOUNG BRITISH ARTISTS

We are looking for any of the artists who exhibited in the Royal Academy's 'Sensation' exhibition of Young British Artists in 1997.

Where artists were exhibited as a pair, we will accept either or both names.

Note. The artists featured in the exhibition all work in the UK but may not necessarily be British in the strict sense of the word.

ABIGAIL LANE	0	LANGLANDS & BELL	0
ADAM CHODZKO	0	MARC QUINN	0
ALAIN MILLER	0	MARCUS HARVEY	1
ALEX HARTLEY	0	MARK FRANCIS	0
CERITH WYN EVANS	0	MARK WALLINGER	0
CHRIS OFILI	0	MARTIN MALONEY	0
DAMIEN HIRST	5	MAT COLLISHAW	0
DARREN ALMOND	0	MICHAEL LANDY	0
DINOS CHAPMAN	1	MONA HATOUM	0
FIONA RAE	2	PAUL FINNEGAN	0
GARY HUME	1	PETER DAVIES	0
GAVIN TURK	0	RACHEL WHITEREAD	0
GILLIAN WEARING	0	RICHARD BILLINGHAM	0
GLEN BROWN	1	RICHARD PATTERSON	0
HADRIAN PIGOTT	0	RON MUECK	0
JAKE CHAPMAN	1	SAM TAYLOR-WOOD	0
JAMES RIELLY	0	SARAH LUCAS	0
JANE SIMPSON	0	SIMON CALLERY	0
JASON MARTIN	0	SIMON PATTERSON	0
JENNY SAVILLE	1	TRACEY EMIN	19
JONATHAN PARSONS	0	YINKA SHONIBARE	0
KEITH COVENTRY	0		

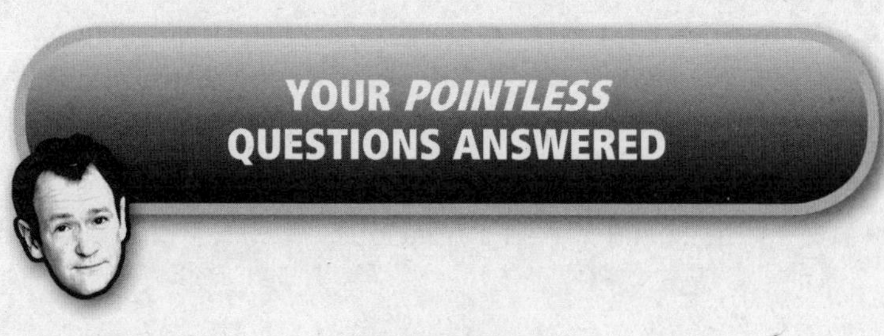

The Chase

What do you think of *The Chase*?

We love *The Chase*. We love Bradley, we love all the people who work on it, we love the show itself. It just happens to be our rival in the schedules, the City to our United if you like (or vice versa if you don't like), so therefore we hate it.

Really? That's a bit extreme.

I'm only joking. We love it. Seriously we do.

Now you're over-egging it. Do you ever meet them?

We used to see them from time to time at the odd show-biz event and there'd always be some good-natured *badinage*. But now they have moved in next to us at Elstree and we see them every day in the corridor. It's all very friendly, and then we go into our respective studios to do quizbattle.

Quizbattle?

Yup. But we have a bit of fun. Bradley sometimes comes in between rounds and sits in Richard's chair, and then Richard goes into Bradley's computer accounts and lays waste to his social life. It's hilarious.

BERRIES

We are looking for the name of any plant, or fruit of a plant, that has its own entry in the Oxford Dictionary of English, whose name ends in the letters 'B-E-R-R-Y'.

We are only looking for one-word answers. So we will not accept 'Goji Berry' for example.

The berries do not have to be edible ones. Obviously we will not be accepting 'berry' itself.

BANEBERRY	0
BARBERRY	1
BAYBERRY	0
BEARBERRY	2
BILBERRY	8
BLACKBERRY	84
BLAEBERRY	3
BLUEBERRY	73
BOYSENBERRY	3
BUNCHBERRY	0
CANDLEBERRY	0
CHECKERBERRY	0
CHINABERRY	0
CHOKEBERRY	0
CLOUDBERRY	5
CORALBERRY	0
COWBERRY	0
CRANBERRY	28
CROWBERRY	1
DEWBERRY	1
DOGBERRY	0
ELDERBERRY	16
FARKLEBERRY	0
FENBERRY	0
GALLBERRY	0
GOOSEBERRY	61
HACKBERRY	0
HUCKLEBERRY	0
INKBERRY	0
JUNEBERRY	0
LINGONBERRY	2
LOGANBERRY	60
MULBERRY	6
NASEBERRY	0
PARTRIDGEBERRY	0
PEABERRY	0
RASPBERRY	87
SALMONBERRY	0
SERVICEBERRY	0
SILVERBERRY	0
SNOWBERRY	1
SOAPBERRY	0
SQUASHBERRY	0
STRAWBERRY	92
TAYBERRY	8
THIMBLEBERRY	0
VEITCHBERRY	0
WAXBERRY	0
WHORTLEBERRY	4
WINEBERRY	1
WINTERBERRY	0
WOLFBERRY	3
YOUNGBERRY	0

COVER VERSIONS

We are going to show you twelve pairs of artists. The second one of each pair has reached the Top 40 in the UK with a cover version of the first artist's song. We would like you to give us the name of the song. We have given you the year in which the COVER VERSION charted in brackets.

PAUL McCARTNEY AND WINGS/GUNS N' ROSES (1991)

TOM WAITS/ROD STEWART (1990)

THE BEE GEES/TAKE THAT (1996)

DOLLY PARTON/THE WHITE STRIPES (2004)

SNOW PATROL/LEONA LEWIS (2008)

THE ZUTONS/AMY WINEHOUSE (2007)

...Continued

COVER VERSIONS

BOB MARLEY/ERIC CLAPTON (1974)

PUBLIC ENEMY/TRICKY (1995)

THE BEATLES/JOE COCKER (1968)

OTIS REDDING/ARETHA FRANKLIN (1967)

LEONARD COHEN/ALEXANDRA BURKE (2008)

NEIL DIAMOND/UB40 (1983)

I SHOT THE SHERRIFF	13
BLACK STEEL	2
WITH A LITTLE HELP FROM MY FRIENDS	26
RESPECT	6
HALLELUJAH	31
RED RED WINE	25

CHILDREN'S TELEVISION

We have mixed up the titles of five popular children's television programmes which aired on the BBC between its inception and today. We want you to unscramble them and tell us what they are.

TERRIBLE IRISH OOHS

PASS BUG

WONDER SUN

ALCOHOL SPY

GIN UP

MALE FRENCH OPEN WINNERS

We are looking for any player who has won a post-war French Open Men's Singles title, that is from 1946 to 2010 inclusive.

ADRIANO PANATTA	0	KEN ROSEWALL	0
ALBERT COSTA	1	LEWIS HOAD	0
ANDRE AGASSI	40	MANUEL SANTANA	0
ANDRES GIMENO	0	MARCEL BERNARD	0
ANDRES GOMEZ	0	MATS WILANDER	1
BJORN BORG	24	MERVYN ROSE	0
BUDGE PATTY	0	MICHAEL CHANG	4
CARLOS MOYA	2	NICOLA PIETRANGELI	0
FRANK PARKER	0	RAFAEL NADAL	48
FRED STOLLE	0	ROD LAVER	4
GASTÓN GAUDIO	3	ROGER FEDERER	49
GUILLERMO VILAS	0	ROY EMERSON	0
GUSTAVO KUERTEN	6	SERGI BRUGUERA	1
ILIE NASTASE	4	SVEN DAVIDSON	0
IVAN LENDL	10	THOMAS MUSTER	3
JAN KODES	0	TONY ROCHE	0
JAROSLAV DROBNY	0	TONY TRABERT	0
JIM COURIER	4	YANNICK NOAH	0
JOZSEF ASBOTH	0	YEVGENY KAFELNIKOV	1
JUAN CARLOS FERRERO	5		

YOUR *POINTLESS* QUESTIONS ANSWERED

Kids' version of *Pointless*

Why don't you do a kids' version of *Pointless*? It would be amazing!

I know, I love how many kids watch the show, and how brilliant they are with facts and lists. It would be perfect.

Then why don't you?

For reasons I've never quite fully understood the BBC are not allowed to.

What are the reasons?

It's either that the BBC as an organization hates children and wants them to be unhappy, or it's a health and safety and insurance issue. But I promise we keep suggesting it.

If you do make it can I get royalties for coming up with the idea?

No, because you are the four-millionth person to suggest it.

Ok, how about a 'late-night' rude version of *Pointless*?

You are the twelve-millionth person to suggest that.

***Pointless* with animals?**

Ok, you're the first person to suggest that.

A team of badgers against a team of horses, two pigs and a duck and a rabbit who met at work?

I will ring the BBC and the RSPCA immediately.

CELEBRITIES WITH DOUBLE INITIALS

We are about to show you fourteen clues about actors and musicians, who all have first names and surnames that start with the same letter. We would like you to use the facts to try and name the celebrities. We want the names the celebrities are most commonly known by.

Oscar and Tony award winner, married to Phoebe Cates

Model, married Richard Gere in 1991

Born in Tennessee, sang 'Simply the Best' in 1989

One-sixth of the 'Friends' main cast

Played Juliet in the 2003 film, 'Love Actually'

Creator, writer and star of the Austin Powers films

Born 1986, star of 'Mean Girls'

KEVIN KLINE	**4**
CINDY CRAWFORD	**17**
TINA TURNER	**60**
COURTENEY COX	**20**
KEIRA KNIGHTLEY	**7**
MIKE MYERS	**38**
LINDSAY LOHAN	**21**

...Continued

CELEBRITIES WITH DOUBLE INITIALS

'The X Factor' winner in 2006

Born 1947, played Jill Munroe in 'Charlie's Angels'

Married Blake Lively in September 2012

Director and star of the 2010 film 'The Expendables'

Played Benjamin Franklin Pierce in M*A*S*H from 1972

Born 1889, starred in 'City Lights' and 'The Great Dictator'

Starred in the 1996 film 'Twister'

LEONA LEWIS 23

FARRAH FAWCETT 13

RYAN REYNOLDS 5

SYLVESTER STALLONE 27

ALAN ALDA 17

CHARLIE CHAPLIN 40

HELEN HUNT 9

RAILWAY STATIONS WITH STREET IN THEIR NAME

We would like you to name any national rail station in England, Scotland or Wales that includes the word 'street' in its name. The word can appear anywhere in the name.

This is according to the Office of Rail Regulation's estimates of station usage 2011–2012. Where stations share the same name, we need the name of the town or city it is in.

Station	Count
ARGYLE STREET	2
BIRMINGHAM MOOR STREET	5
BIRMINGHAM NEW STREET	36
BLAKE STREET	0
CANNON STREET	5
CARDIFF QUEEN STREET	1
CHESTER-LE-STREET	4
CLAPHAM HIGH STREET	1
DUKE STREET	0
FENCHURCH STREET	26
GLASGOW QUEEN STREET	2
GOLF STREET	0
HAM STREET	0
HIGH STREET	0
LIVERPOOL JAMES STREET	1
LIVERPOOL LIME STREET	29
LIVERPOOL STREET	38
OLD STREET	5
PAISLEY GILMOUR STREET	0
PARK STREET	1
PARSON STREET	2
SHOREDITCH HIGH STREET	0
SILVER STREET	1
SMETHWICK ROLFE STREET	0
SOLE STREET	1
ST JAMES STREET	1
STREETHOUSE	0
TURKEY STREET	1
WATFORD HIGH STREET	0
WOOD STREET	0
WORCESTER FOREGATE STREET	0

RAF AIRCRAFT DURING WWII

Here are five anagrams which, when solved, will give the names of RAF aircraft in use during World War II. We would like you to unscramble the anagrams and tell us the names of the aircraft.

In each case, we've given the common short-form names of the aircraft.

RAUNCHIER

GOLD TIARA

QUITS MOO

RIPE FIST

A RADAR CUB

HURRICANE	**21**
GLADIATOR	**1**
MOSQUITO	**58**
SPITFIRE	**68**
BARRACUDA	**6**

BOOKS BY PHILIP PULLMAN

We're looking for the titles of any of the novels or children's books written by Philip Pullman, up to the end of September 2012. Where his novels are published as part of a trilogy or quartet, we are not looking for the blanket name of the trilogy or quartet. However, we will accept the titles of any of the individual novels within them.

We won't accept his published plays.

CLOCKWORK	4
COUNT KARLSTEIN	0
GALATEA	0
HOW TO BE COOL	0
I WAS A RAT!	3
LYRA'S OXFORD	0
MOSSYCOAT	0
NORTHERN LIGHTS	17
ONCE UPON A TIME IN THE NORTH	0
PUSS IN BOOTS	0
SPRING-HEELED JACK	0
THE AMBER SPYGLASS	7
THE BROKEN BRIDGE	0
THE BUTTERFLY TATTOO	1
THE FIREWORK-MAKER'S DAUGHTER	1
THE GAS-FITTERS' BALL	0
THE GOOD MAN JESUS AND THE SCOUNDREL CHRIST	0
THE HAUNTED STORM	1
THE RUBY IN THE SMOKE	3
THE SCARECROW AND HIS SERVANT	0
THE SHADOW IN THE NORTH	0
THE SUBTLE KNIFE	5
THE TIGER IN THE WELL	3
THE TIN PRINCESS	1
THE WONDERFUL STORY OF ALADDIN AND THE ENCHANTED LAMP	0
THUNDERBOLT'S WAXWORK	0

YOUR *POINTLESS* QUESTIONS ANSWERED

Shirts

We were wondering about your shirts?

What about them?

Where do they come from?

Oh phew. That is an excellent question. I'll just go and find out.

[PAUSE]

Just been to Wardrobe. To ask and . . . They um . . .

It's ok, take your time.

Thanks.

Glass of water?

Yes please. Sharon in Wardrobe . . . Just get my breath . . . Sharon says . . . Gets a new batch every couple of series . . . Come from Emmett, Eton and somewhere else. Erm, I had it . . . no it's gone. Wait here, I'll be back in a sec.

[PAUSE]

Thomas Pink.

So are they yours?

Not really. Sorry, just give me a minute. It just said '[PAUSE]' back there when I ran off, like Wardrobe's round the corner, but it's not, it's bloody miles away. Sorry, where were we? Oh yes. I mean they *are* mine. No-one else wears them. But I don't take them home; they live in the *Pointless* wardrobe. I wouldn't really need that many smart shirts at home.

Why? How many are there?

No idea. Fifteen? A couple of years ago Richard and I lost about a stone and a half each and Sharon had to get smaller suits and shirts for both of us. I wonder if she's kept the old ones just in case we pile it all back on again.

A stone and a half's good. How did that happen?

Dunno. All that running back and forth to Wardrobe I expect.

COLD WAR LEADERS

We are going to show you five countries (along with the title of their leader) – we would like you to name any leader of any of these countries throughout the Cold War.

For avoidance of doubt, the 'Cold War', took place between 1946–1989 (inclusive).

We will not accept interim leaders or leaders of provisional governments.

USA (President)

UK (Prime Minister)

West Germany (Chancellor)

USSR (Chairman or First Secretary of the Communist Party)

France (President)

FRANCE (PRESIDENT)

CHARLES DE GAULLE	41
FRANÇOIS MITTERRAND	12
GEORGES POMPIDOU	5
RENÉ COTY	0
VALÉRY GISCARD D'ESTAING	5
VINCENT AURIOL	0

UK (PRIME MINISTER)

ALEC DOUGLAS-HOME	10
ANTHONY EDEN	21
CLEMENT ATTLEE	20
EDWARD HEATH	25
HAROLD MACMILLAN	29
HAROLD WILSON	40
JAMES CALLAGHAN	20
MARGARET THATCHER	46
WINSTON CHURCHILL	50

USA (PRESIDENT)

DWIGHT D. EISENHOWER	16
GEORGE H. W. BUSH	12
GERALD FORD	4
HARRY S. TRUMAN	8
JIMMY CARTER	12
JOHN F. KENNEDY	37
LYNDON B. JOHNSON	11
RICHARD NIXON	19
RONALD REAGAN	18

USSR (GENERAL SECRETARY OF THE CENTRAL COMMITTEE OF THE COMMUNIST PARTY)

GEORGY MALENKOV	0
JOSEPH STALIN	23
KONSTANTIN CHERNENKO	1
LEONID BREZHNEV	10
MIKHAIL GORBACHEV	12
NIKITA KHRUSHCHEV	29
YURI ANDROPOV	8

WEST GERMANY (CHANCELLOR)

HELMUT KOHL	11
HELMUT SCHMIDT	2
KONRAD ADENAUER	11
KURT GEORG KIESINGER	0
LUDWIG ERHARD	0
WILLY BRANDT	14

UK NUMBER ONE ALBUMS WITH ONE-WORD TITLES

We are about to show you twelve UK number one albums along with the year in which they first reached number one – we would like you to tell us who released them please.

ARRIVAL (1977)

STUPIDITY (1976)

RUDEBOX (2006)

THRILLER (1983)

GRACELAND (1986)

LOVESEXY (1988)

ABBA	12
DR. FEELGOOD	1
ROBBIE WILLIAMS	16
MICHAEL JACKSON	80
PAUL SIMON	28
PRINCE	7

...Continued

UK NUMBER ONE ALBUMS WITH ONE-WORD TITLES

ZOOROPA (1993)

STARS (1991)

PARANOID (1970)

CARIBOU (1974)

RUMOURS (1978)

NATURAL (1996)

U2	15
SIMPLY RED	21
BLACK SABBATH	13
ELTON JOHN	4
FLEETWOOD MAC	31
PETER ANDRE	0

EUROPEAN SAUSAGE ORIGINS

We're going to show you the names of five sausages from around Europe. We want you to tell us from which country they traditionally originate.

KRAKOWSKA

FALUKORV

MORTADELLA

BRATWURST

BOUDIN BLANC Á L'ANCIENNE

POLAND **70**

SWEDEN **6**

ITALY **48**

GERMANY **93**

FRANCE **65**

90s FOOTBALL

FA CUP SEMI-FINALISTS

We are looking for the name of any club that made it to the last four of the FA Cup, that is to the semi-finals, played from 1990 to 1999 inclusive.

1999 ARSENAL CHARITY SHIELD SQUAD

We are looking for any member of the 1999 Charity Shield-winning Arsenal squad.

To be clear, we mean any Arsenal footballer who played or sat on the substitutes' bench for the match. The Charity Shield is now known as the Community Shield.

We require first names and surnames, but in the case of a player being more commonly known by just one name, we will accept the more common name.

SCOTTISH FA CUP SEMI-FINALISTS

We are looking for the name of any club that made it to the last four of the Scottish FA Cup, that is to the semi-finals, played from 1990 to 1999 inclusive.

FA CUP SEMI-FINALISTS

ARSENAL	45	NOTTINGHAM FOREST	2
ASTON VILLA	9	OLDHAM ATHLETIC	2
CHELSEA	31	PORTSMOUTH	3
CHESTERFIELD	1	SHEFFIELD UNITED	0
CRYSTAL PALACE	0	SHEFFIELD WEDNESDAY	1
EVERTON	9	SUNDERLAND	0
LIVERPOOL	41	TOTTENHAM HOTSPUR	12
LUTON TOWN	0	WEST HAM UNITED	5
MANCHESTER UNITED	53	WIMBLEDON	1
MIDDLESBROUGH	0	WOLVERHAMPTON WANDERERS	1
NEWCASTLE UNITED	4		
NORWICH CITY	1		

1999 ARSENAL CHARITY SHIELD SQUAD

ALEX MANNINGER	0	NIGEL WINTERBURN	3
CHRISTOPHER WREH	0	NWANKWO KANU	0
EMMANUEL PETIT	0	OLEH LUZHNY	0
FREDRIK LJUNGBERG	0	PAOLO VERNAZZA	0
GILLES GRIMANDI	0	PATRICK VIEIRA	3
JOHN LUKIC	0	RAY PARLOUR	1
LEE DIXON	7	STEFAN MALZ	0
LUIS BOA MORTE	0	STUART TAYLOR	0
MARTIN KEOWN	3	SYLVINHO	0

SCOTTISH FA CUP SEMI-FINALISTS

ABERDEEN	14	HEARTS	16
AIRDRIE	0	HIBERNIAN	16
CELTIC	62	KILMARNOCK	5
CLYDEBANK	0	MOTHERWELL	7
DUNDEE UNITED	6	RANGERS	49
FALKIRK	2	ST JOHNSTONE	0

YOUR *POINTLESS* QUESTIONS ANSWERED

Studio audience

Can I come and watch *Pointless* being recorded live?

You sure can. We have an audience of about 100 people, and they see two shows being recorded. Or one show if it's a *Pointless Celebrities*, because they take much longer to record, due to the fact that celebrities talk more and pay less attention than normal people.

How much do tickets cost? I'm guessing about £75 plus booking fee?

No, they're free!

Get outta town!

I ain't even kidding you. You can apply for tickets online at www.sroaudiences.com.

And is it just like watching the real show?

Pretty much, except Xander and I sometimes say rude things that have to be edited out.

So it's actually BETTER than watching the real show?

Well there are a few downsides. You can't pause the show in the middle to go to the loo, or get up in a boring bit to make a cup of tea. And you're not allowed to shout out answers or openly laugh at what one of the contestants is wearing.

How long do the recordings take?

Each one takes about an hour and a quarter to film, and there's a ten-minute break in the middle for everyone to go and put new clothes on and pretend it's the next day.

Why do recordings take an hour and a quarter when the show is only forty-five minutes?

A combination of three things. 1) Xander and I wittering on and, as previously mentioned, occasionally swearing, 2) resetting all the podiums after each round and 3) we very often get things wrong, due to our inability to be slick television hosts. We have three brilliant warm-up artists, Mark Olver, Finn Taylor and Andrew Bird, one of whom keeps everyone entertained during the breaks.

And where do you film?

Elstree Studios in Borehamwood.

And where is that?

I don't know, I just put it in the satnav every day. Near London I think.

Ok, I'm in. See you next year!

Excellent. Please forgive the swearing.

ROBERT REDFORD FILMS

We are looking for any feature film given a cinema release in the UK or USA for which Robert Redford received either an acting credit or directing credit, or both, up to the start of 2012.

Short films, TV films, documentaries and films in which he played himself do not count. Uncredited appearances do not count and we will only accept the English titles.

A BRIDGE TOO FAR	4
A RIVER RUNS THROUGH IT	9
ALL THE PRESIDENT'S MEN	3
AN UNFINISHED LIFE	0
BAREFOOT IN THE PARK	9
BRUBAKER	3
BUTCH CASSIDY AND THE SUNDANCE KID	36
CHARLOTTE'S WEB	2
DOWNHILL RACER	0
HAVANA	1
HOW TO STEAL A DIAMOND IN FOUR UNEASY LESSONS	1
INDECENT PROPOSAL	15
INSIDE DAISY CLOVER	0
JEREMIAH JOHNSON	1
LEGAL EAGLES	1
LIONS FOR LAMBS	2
LITTLE FAUSS AND BIG HALSY	0
ORDINARY PEOPLE	1
OUT OF AFRICA	8
QUIZ SHOW	0
SITUATION HOPELESS – BUT NOT SERIOUS	0
SNEAKERS	3
SPY GAME	6
TELL THEM WILLIE BOY IS HERE	0
THE CANDIDATE	1
THE CHASE	1
THE CLEARING	1
THE CONSPIRATOR	0
THE ELECTRIC HORSEMAN	0
THE GREAT GATSBY	14
THE GREAT WALDO PEPPER	1
THE HORSE WHISPERER	19
THE LAST CASTLE	2
THE LEGEND OF BAGGER VANCE	0
THE MILAGRO BEANFIELD WAR	0
THE NATURAL	0
THE STING	19
THE WAY WE WERE	3
THIS PROPERTY IS CONDEMNED	0
THREE DAYS OF THE CONDOR	0
UP CLOSE & PERSONAL	0
WAR HUNT	3

AMERICAN FOOTBALL AND BASEBALL TEAMS

We are going to show you 12 pairs of US sports team names.

Each pair consists firstly of the name of an American Football team followed by that of a baseball team, both of which play in the same city.

We would like you to tell us the name of the US city that has teams with those names.

The American Football teams are all National Football League teams, and the baseball teams are all Major League teams, as of their respective sports seasons that end in 2012.

49ers / Giants

Texans / Astros

Bears / Cubs

Eagles / Phillies

Seahawks / Mariners

Rams / Cardinals

SAN FRANCISCO	17
HOUSTON	6
CHICAGO	36
PHILADELPHIA	40
SEATTLE	14
ST. LOUIS	3

...Continued

AMERICAN FOOTBALL AND BASEBALL TEAMS

Redskins / Nationals

Raiders / Athletics

Dolphins / Marlins

Browns / Indians

Chiefs / Royals

Steelers / Pirates

WASHINGTON	16
OAKLAND	1
MIAMI	38
CLEVELAND	13
KANSAS CITY	5
PITTSBURGH	23

FAMOUS PHYSICISTS

We are going to show you the names of five famous physicists, along with their dates of birth. However, we have removed alternate letters in each of their names. We would like you to fill in the blanks.

B _ I _ N C _ X (1968)

R _ C _ A _ D F _ Y _ M _ N (1918)

E _ N _ S _ R _ T _ E _ F _ R _ (1871)

A _ B _ R _ E _ N _ T _ I _ (1879)

M _ R _ E C _ R _ E (1867)

BRIAN COX	42
RICHARD FEYNMAN	10
ERNEST RUTHERFORD	12
ALBERT EINSTEIN	58
MARIE CURIE	31

VETERAN CROONERS

PERRY COMO SINGLES

We are looking for the title of any single by Perry Como which reached the Top 40 in the UK chart up to the end of October 2013. We will accept collaborations. Double A-sides will be counted as separate answers.

TONY BENNETT SINGLES

We are looking for the title of any single by Tony Bennett which reached the Top 40 in the UK chart, up to the end of October 2013. We will accept collaborations. Double A-sides will be counted as separate answers.

FRANKIE VAUGHAN SINGLES

We are looking for the title of any single by Frankie Vaughan which reached the Top 40 in the UK chart, up to the end of October 2013. We will accept collaborations. Double A-sides will be counted as separate answers.

PERRY COMO SINGLES

Song	Score
AND I LOVE YOU SO	0
CATCH A FALLING STAR	11
CATERINA	0
DELAWARE	1
DON'T LET THE STARS GET IN YOUR EYES	1
FOR THE GOOD TIMES	0
GLENDORA	0
HOT DIGGITY (DOG ZIGGITY BOOM)	0
I KNOW	0
I MAY NEVER PASS THIS WAY AGAIN	0
I THINK OF YOU	0
I WANT TO GIVE	0
IDLE GOSSIP	0
IT'S IMPOSSIBLE	0
JUKE BOX BABY	0
KEWPIE DOLL	0
LOVE MAKES THE WORLD GO ROUND	0
MAGIC MOMENTS	8
MANDOLINS IN THE MOONLIGHT	0
MOON TALK	0
MORE	0
PAPA LOVES MAMBO	3
TINA MARIE	0
TOMBOY	0
WALK RIGHT BACK	0
WANTED	0

TONY BENNETT SINGLES

Song	Score
BODY AND SOUL	1
CLOSE YOUR EYES	0
COME NEXT SPRING	0
I LEFT MY HEART IN SAN FRANCISCO	18
IF I RULED THE WORLD	0
STRANGER IN PARADISE	1
THE GOOD LIFE	3
THE VERY THOUGHT OF YOU	0
TILL	0

FRANKIE VAUGHAN SINGLES

AM I WASTING MY TIME ON YOU	0
CAN'T GET ALONG WITHOUT YOU	0
COME SOFTLY TO ME	0
DON'T STOP TWIST	0
GOTTA HAVE SOMETHING IN THE BANK FRANK	0
HAPPY DAYS AND LONELY NIGHTS	0
HELLO DOLLY	0
HEY MAMA	0
ISTANBUL (NOT CONSTANTINOPLE)	0
KEWPIE DOLL	0
KISSES SWEETER THAN WINE	1
KOOKIE LITTLE PARADISE	0
LOOP-DE-LOOP	0
MAN ON FIRE	1
MILORD	0
MY BOY FLAT TOP	1
NEVERTHELESS	0
SEVENTEEN	1
SO TIRED	1
THAT'S MY DOLL	0
THE GARDEN OF EDEN	1
THE GREEN DOOR	16
THE HEART OF A MAN	0
THERE MUST BE A WAY	0
TOWER OF STRENGTH	2
TWEEDLE DEE	0
WALKIN' TALL	1
WANDERIN' EYES	0
WE ARE NOT ALONE	0
WHAT MORE DO YOU WANT	0
WONDERFUL THINGS	0

Repeats

Why does the BBC show repeats?

That's because we only make about 180 daytime shows a year, and there are 261 weekdays in a year. Take ten days out for Wimbledon fortnight and a bunch of bank holidays here and there and that's 237 days, which means that 57 days are going to have to be filled with repeats.

Then why don't you just make more shows?

Good question. The filming wouldn't be a problem, although it would probably start to interfere with Richard's exciting plans in the Far East,* it's more the amount of time the Question Team need to make sure each round of each show is brilliant because of course every single question has to be fully researched.

What kind of research do you mean?

* He's building a massive hideaway underneath an island just off the coast of Malaysia – best not say any more, you'll discover soon enough.

Well 180 shows need 720 separate rounds, so at the very least that means giving 72,000 people 72,000 seconds to come up with their answers. That can't happen in the blink of an eye . . .

So we just have to put up with repeats every so often?

Or you could think of it like this: fifty-seven days a year we are giving you a second chance to find a pointless answer.

FIRST NAMES OF FASHION DESIGNERS

We're going to show you the surnames of famous fashion designers, along with their year of birth. We'd like you to give us their first names please.

RICCI (1883)

VIONNET (1876)

DIOR (1905)

HERRERA (1939)

AMIES (1909)

WANG (1949)

SAINT LAURENT (1936)

NINA	48
MADELEINE	0
CHRISTIAN	76
CAROLINA	1
HARDY	62
VERA	31
YVES	91

...Continued

FIRST NAMES OF FASHION DESIGNERS

SCHIAPARELLI (1890)

CAVALLI (1940)

CASSINI (1913)

CHANEL (1883)

WESTWOOD (1941)

LAGERFELD (1938)

HARTNELL (1901)

ELSA	1
ROBERTO	8
OLEG	0
COCO	75
VIVIENNE	86
KARL	45
NORMAN	50

GREEK FOOD

The correct answers here are all dishes or ingredients typically associated with Greek cuisine. The incorrect answers will not be foods at all.

TZATZIKI

STIFADO

SIRTAKI

DOLMATHAKIA

YEMISTA

SOUVLAKI

MOUSSAKA

TZATZIKI	15
STIFADO	4
SIRTAKI	X
DOLMATHAKIA	0
YEMISTA	0
SOUVLAKI	6
MOUSSAKA	45

...Continued

GREEK FOOD

KEFTETHES

PASTITSIO

PANAYIOTOU

KLEFTIKO

FETA

TARAMASALATA

TSOLIADES

KEFTETHES	0
PASTITSIO	1
PANAYIOTOU	X
KLEFTIKO	5
FETA	25
TARAMASALATA	15
TSOLIADES	X

SONGS FROM 'CHITTY CHITTY BANG BANG'

Any song on the original soundtrack recording of the film 'Chitty Chitty Bang Bang', excluding 'Chitty Chitty Bang Bang' itself and the main title music.

CHU-CHI FACE 3

DOLL ON A MUSIC BOX 0

HUSHABYE MOUNTAIN 2

LOVELY LONELY MAN 0

ME OL' BAMBOO 2

POSH 6

THE ROSES OF SUCCESS 0

TOOT SWEETS 13

TRULY SCRUMPTIOUS 17

YOU TWO 1

ENGLAND CRICKETERS NOT BORN IN ENGLAND

Any cricketer who has represented England at One Day Internationals or Test matches since January 1980, up to the beginning of April 2011, who was not born in England.

ADAM HOLLIOAKE	0
ALLAN LAMB	4
AMJAD KHAN	0
ANDREW STRAUSS	3
ANDY CADDICK	0
BEN HOLLIOAKE	0
BOB WOOLMER	0
CHRIS LEWIS	0
CHRIS SMITH	0
DEREK PRINGLE	0
DERMOT REEVE	0
DEVON MALCOLM	0
DOUGIE BROWN	0
ED JOYCE	0
EOIN MORGAN	2
GERAINT JONES	1
GLADSTONE SMALL	0
GRAEME HICK	1
IAN GREIG	0
JASON GALLIAN	0
JOEY BENJAMIN	0
JONATHAN TROTT	6
KEVIN PIETERSEN	22
MARTIN McCAGUE	0
MATT PRIOR	2
MIN PATEL	0
NASSER HUSSEIN	1
NEAL RADFORD	0
NEIL WILLIAMS	0
NORMAN COWANS	0
OWAIS SHAH	0
PAUL PARKER	0
PAUL TERRY	0
PHIL EDMONDS	0
PHILLIP DEFREITAS	0
ROBERT CROFT	0
ROBIN JACKMAN	0
ROBIN SMITH	0
ROLAND BUTCHER	0
SIMON JONES	0
TIM AMBROSE	0
USMAN AFZAAL	0
WILF SLACK	0

YOUR *POINTLESS* QUESTIONS ANSWERED

You and Xander

Do you and Xander actually get along in real life?

Yes. Well I get on with him at least. You'd have to ask him if he gets along with me, and you can't do that at the moment because he's at Ben Miller's house having dinner.

How long have you and Xander known each other?

We met at university when we were eighteen, so nearly ten or eleven years now.

Whatever Richard. Is he as nice as he seems?

He is, I'm afraid. He's one of the nicest men I've ever met. It's sickening isn't it?

And does he really know the answers to all the questions or does someone tell him?

He just knows them, he's very clever. There are certain subjects however where I won't ask him to fill in the board. I know that while he can rattle off all the answers for eighteenth-century literature or 90s music, he fares less well on, say, post-war World Snooker champions. Occasionally there will be a round of questions and I will see his little eyes light up like an excited child and I'll know he wants to give all the answers. Other times a subject comes up and he refuses to make eye-contact, like a man who has got on a late-night bus and wishes he hadn't, and then I know not to ask him.

And why does he say everyone has been 'brilliant' even when they've scored 200 points by giving the answers 'Peter Shilton' and 'Anne of Cleves' for David Bowie albums?

Because he's a nice man and believes that everybody should be treated with kindness and respect.

My Uncle Ron has already scored 100 points 17 times going through this book. Would Xander call him 'brilliant'?

Ok, I suppose there are exceptions.

CAPITAL CITIES AND THEIR RIVERS

We're going to show you the names of fourteen rivers which flow through national capital cities. We want you to name the capital city which they flow through.

KIFISSOS

SPREE

VANTAA

VISTULA

LIFFEY

BARADA

SEINE

ATHENS	21
BERLIN	13
HELSINKI	1
WARSAW	4
DUBLIN	52
DAMASCUS	2
PARIS	84

...Continued

CAPITAL CITIES AND THEIR RIVERS

MOLONGLO

RIMAC

VLTAVA

AMSTEL

TIBER

HAN

THAMES

CANBERRA	0
LIMA	2
PRAGUE	4
AMSTERDAM	42
ROME	38
SEOUL	3
LONDON	95

WOMEN WHO MARRIED MORE THAN ONCE

We are going to show you a list of six famous women; we would like you to give us the name of any of their husbands up to the beginning of October 2012.

MARILYN MONROE

MELANIE GRIFFITH

JOAN COLLINS

MADONNA

KATIE PRICE

PRINCESS ANNE

PRINCESS ANNE	
MARK PHILLIPS	46
TIMOTHY LAURENCE	3
MELANIE GRIFFITH	
ANTONIO BANDERAS	13
DON JOHNSON	11
STEVE BAUER	1
MARILYN MONROE	
ARTHUR MILLER	13
JIMMY DOUGHERTY	0
JOE DIMAGGIO	12
MADONNA	
GUY RITCHIE	26
SEAN PENN	24
KATIE PRICE	
ALEX REID	16
PETER ANDRE	53
JOAN COLLINS	
ANTHONY NEWLEY	11
MAXWELL REED	2
PERCY GIBSON	2
PETER HOLM	3
RON KASS	4

POTATO VARIETIES

We are going to show you the names of five varieties of potato; however, we have mashed them up. We'd like you to unscramble the anagram you think the fewest of our 100 knew. To help you we are indicating the number of words the variety consists of.

DONGLE DOWNER (2 words)

PAMPER IRIS (2 words)

I STEAM (1 word)

SO RETRO (1 word)

NEW DARK DIG (2 words)

GOLDEN WONDER	3
MARIS PIPER	59
ESTIMA	6
ROOSTER	15
KING EDWARD	37

AUTHORS IN THE BBC 'BIG READ' TOP 100

In 2003, the BBC conducted a poll to find the nation's best loved novel – The Big Read. We're looking for any author who had one or more books voted into the top 100.

Where a book has been written by more than one author, both names will count as separate answers.

Author	Count
A.A. Milne	1
Aldous Huxley	0
Alexandre Dumas	0
Anna Sewell	0
Anya Seton	0
Arthur Golden	0
Arthur Ransome	0
Arundhati Roy	0
C.S. Lewis	4
Charles Dickens	17
Charlotte Brontë	3
Colleen McCullough	0
Dan Brown	0
Daphne du Maurier	1
Dodie Smith	0
Donna Tartt	0
Douglas Adams	0
Emily Brontë	5
Enid Blyton	4
Eoin Colfer	0
Evelyn Waugh	2
F. Scott Fitzgerald	1
Frances Hodgson Burnett	0
Frank Herbert	0
Fyodor Dostoyevsky	0
Gabriel García Márquez	0
George Eliot	1
George Orwell	3
Harper Lee	3
Helen Fielding	0
J.D. Salinger	1
J.K. Rowling	30
J.R.R. Tolkien	13
Jack Kerouac	0
Jacqueline Wilson	3
James Joyce	0
Jane Austen	11
Jean M. Auel	0
Jeffrey Archer	3
John Fowles	0
John Irving	1
John Steinbeck	3
Joseph Heller	0
Ken Follett	0
Kenneth Grahame	0
L.M. Montgomery	0
Leo Tolstoy	3
Lewis Carroll	1
Louis de Bernières	0
Louis Sachar	0
Louisa May Alcott	0
Malorie Blackman	0
Margaret Mitchell	0
Mario Puzo	0
Meg Cabot	0
Mervyn Peake	0
Michelle Magorian	0
Neil Gaiman	0
Nevil Shute	1
Patrick Suskind	0
Paulo Coelho	0
Philip Pullman	1
Raymond E. Feist	0
Richard Adams	0
Roald Dahl	5
Robert Louis Stevenson	1
Robert Tressell	0
Rosamunde Pilcher	1
Salman Rushdie	0
Sebastian Faulks	2
Stella Gibbons	0
Stephen King	7
Terry Pratchett	4
Thomas Hardy	2
Vikram Seth	0
Wilkie Collins	0
William Golding	2

YOUR *POINTLESS* QUESTIONS ANSWERED

'As we'll ever be'

When you ask the finalists if they're ready, why do they always say 'as we'll ever be'?

Interesting. That's not actually what they're saying. They're really saying 'as Wear, Lever "B"'. In the 30s under Ludwig Blattner's ownership, Elstree Studios was divided up into sectors named after British rivers. Wear was the hospitality block. In a bid to cut studio costs, Blattner was famous for throwing the switch on the 'B' Circuit of Wear's junction box at any moment, plunging the bars and hospitality suites into inky blackness. Hence 'As Wear, lever "B"', which is Elstree argot for 'Yes Xander, we're ready to go at any moment.'

See also 'Tyne to shut up.'

NINETEENTH & TWENTIETH-CENTURY EVENTS AND THEIR DECADES

These events all occurred in either the nineteenth or twentieth century. We are looking for the decades in which these events took place.

UK FOOD RATIONING ENDED AFTER WORLD WAR II

LUMIÈRE BROTHERS' FIRST PUBLIC FILM SHOWING

FIRST BRITISH FEMALE PRIME MINISTER

CALIFORNIA GOLDRUSH BEGINS

FALL OF THE BERLIN WALL

NAPOLEON DIES ON ST HELENA

SCOTTISH PARLIAMENT FOUNDED

1950s	42
1890s	8
1970s	58
1840s	9
1980s	49
1820s	9
1990s	17

...Continued

NINETEENTH & TWENTIETH-CENTURY EVENTS AND THEIR DECADES

FIRST SUCCESSFUL TEST TUBE BABY BORN

KRAKATOA'S MAJOR ERUPTION

ENGLAND WIN THE FIFA WORLD CUP

QUEEN VICTORIA BORN

HONG KONG RETURNED TO CHINA

HOWARD CARTER DISCOVERS TUTANKHAMUN'S TOMB

FIRST BRITISH WOMEN GIVEN THE RIGHT TO VOTE

1970s	31
1880s	4
1960s	82
1810s	7
1990s	50
1920s	14
1910s	8

ACTORS AND THEIR BEST AND WORST PERFORMANCES

We are about to show you a list of actors on the board. We'd like you to name any film for which any of them received an Oscar nomination or a Razzie nomination in an acting category up to and including the ceremonies held in 2012 – this includes films for which they won.

To clarify, for the Razzies, any category which honours ACTING in film will count here – including Razzies such as 'Worst Screen Couple' or 'Worst New Star' – however other awards for directing, writing etc., will not.

The actors are:

BRAD PITT

GEORGE CLOONEY

JOHN TRAVOLTA

JULIA ROBERTS

NICOLE KIDMAN

SHARON STONE

BRAD PITT (Oscar)	
Moneyball	3
The Curious Case of Benjamin Button	3
Twelve Monkeys	1
BRAD PITT (Razzie)	
Interview with the Vampire: The Vampire Chronicles	0
GEORGE CLOONEY (Oscar)	
Michael Clayton	0
Syriana	1
The Descendants	4
Up in the Air	0
GEORGE CLOONEY (Razzie)	
Batman & Robin	0
JOHN TRAVOLTA (Oscar)	
Pulp Fiction	11
Saturday Night Fever	17
JOHN TRAVOLTA (Razzie)	
Battlefield Earth: A Saga of the Year 3000	2
Domestic Disturbance	0
Lucky Numbers	0
Old Dogs	0
Perfect	0
Shout	0
Staying Alive	1
Swordfish	0
The Experts	0
Two of a Kind	0
JULIA ROBERTS (Oscar)	
Erin Brockovich	17
Pretty Woman	38
Steel Magnolias	1
JULIA ROBERTS (Razzie)	
Hook	0
Mary Reilly	0
NICOLE KIDMAN (Oscar)	
Moulin Rouge!	7
Rabbit Hole	1
The Hours	2
NICOLE KIDMAN (Razzie)	
Bewitched	1
Just Go With It	0
SHARON STONE (Oscar)	
Casino	2
SHARON STONE (Razzie)	
Allan Quatermain and the Lost City of Gold	0
Basic Instinct	17
Basic Instinct 2	2
Catwoman	0
Diabolique	0
Gloria	0
Intersection	0
Last Dance	0
Sliver	3
The Specialist	0

TREES

We are going to show you five anagrams of the names of trees which are commonly found in the UK. We want you to tell us what they are.

CABAL PREP

NUZZLE ME POKY

STENCH SHOUTER

CRIB SHRIVEL

ACE MR SOY

CRAB APPLE	14
MONKEY PUZZLE	21
HORSE CHESTNUT	12
SILVER BIRCH	16
SYCAMORE	23

ABBA

ABBA SPOUSES

We are looking for the name of any individual who has ever married one of the four members of ABBA.

MAMMA MIA! CAST

We are looking for the name of any actor or actress who received an acting credit for playing a named character in the 2008 film 'Mamma Mia!', as listed by the IMDB. By named character, we mean that we will not accept actors who played 'Stag' or 'Hen'.

ABBA GOLD

We are looking for the title of any track on 'ABBA GOLD', which, in October 2012, was declared by the Official Charts Company to be the best-selling CD of all time in the UK.

We are only including tracks on the original UK release of the album, not releases elsewhere or later bonus CDs.

ABBA SPOUSES

AGNETHA FÄLTSKOG	8	MONA NÖRKLIT	0
ANNI-FRID LYNGSTAD	9	PRINCE RUZZO REUSS VON PLAUEN	0
BENNY ANDERSSON	16	RAGNAR FREDRIKSSON	0
BJÖRN ULVAEUS	21	TOMAS SONNENFELD	0
LENA KÄLLERSJÖ	0		

MAMMA MIA! CAST

AMANDA SEYFRIED	16	JANE FOUFAS	0
ASHLEY LILLEY	0	JUAN PABLO DI PACE	0
CHRIS JARVIS	0	JULIE WALTERS	18
CHRISTINE BARANSKI	1	LEONIE HILL	0
COLIN DAVIS	0	MARIA LOPIANO	0
COLIN FIRTH	15	MERYL STREEP	49
DOMINIC COOPER	1	MIA SOTERIOU	0
ENZO SQUILLINO JR	0	MYRA MCFADYEN	0
GEORGE GEORGIOU	0	NANCY BALDWIN	0
HEATHER EMMANUEL	0	NIALL BUGGY	0
HEMI YEROHAM	0	NORMA ATALLAH	0

PHILIP MICHAEL 0

PIERCE BROSNAN 49

RACHEL MCDOWALL 0

RICARDO MONTEZ 0

STELLAN SKARSGÅRD 1

ABBA GOLD

CHIQUITITA 2

DANCING QUEEN 44

DOES YOUR MOTHER KNOW 2

FERNANDO 16

GIMME! GIMME! GIMME! (A MAN AFTER MIDNIGHT) 5

I HAVE A DREAM 0

KNOWING ME, KNOWING YOU 9

LAY ALL YOUR LOVE ON ME 0

MAMMA MIA 47

MONEY, MONEY, MONEY 16

ONE OF US 0

S.O.S. 9

SUPER TROUPER 4

TAKE A CHANCE ON ME 3

THANK YOU FOR THE MUSIC 5

THE NAME OF THE GAME 0

THE WINNER TAKES IT ALL 13

VOULEZ-VOUS 3

WATERLOO 56

YOUR *POINTLESS* QUESTIONS ANSWERED

Would you ever be contestants?

Would you and Xander ever appear as contestants?

We do get asked this a lot. We would definitely like to. It would have to be for a special occasion though.

Do you think you would win?

I would hope so. We have learned so much over the years about chemical elements, and they always come up.

What would . . .

Rutherfordium.

I haven't asked a . . .

Lawrencium.

We're not talking about . . .

Einsteinium.

Ok, ok. But you're saying that one day you will appear as contestants?

Yes.

And who would present the show?

I think that Stephen Fry should be me and Victoria Wood should be Xander.

That would be amazing!

Wouldn't it just?

In fact, why don't they just host it all the time? That would be much better!

. . .

Richard?

Copernicium.

BRITISH DARTS CHAMPIONS

Any male British darts player who has won either the BDO or the PDC World Championships (or both) since the inception of each event in 1978 and 1994 (respectively), up to and including the 2012 events.

By 'British', for the purpose of this question, we mean having been born in or representing the UK.

ADRIAN LEWIS	9
ANDY FORDHAM	2
BOB ANDERSON	3
DENNIS PRIESTLEY	3
ERIC BRISTOW	38
JOCKY WILSON	25
JOHN LOWE	24
JOHN WALTON	1
KEITH DELLER	12
LEIGHTON REES	7
LES WALLACE	3
MARK WEBSTER	2
MARTIN ADAMS	6
PHIL TAYLOR	26
RICHIE BURNETT	3
STEVE BEATON	1
TED HANKEY	4

CHEESES OF THE WORLD

We are going to show you the names of twelve types of cheese. We would like you to tell us the country where that cheese was originally made or with which it is most commonly associated.

BRIE

RABAÇAL

MANCHEGO

JARLSBERG

GORGONZOLA

ASADERO

FRANCE	94
PORTUGAL	2
SPAIN	22
NORWAY	12
ITALY	63
MEXICO	3

...Continued

CHEESES OF THE WORLD

HARZER KÄSE

MONTEREY JACK

GOUDA

BALATON

EMMENTAL

HAVARTI

GERMANY	14
USA	41
NETHERLANDS	67
HUNGARY	3
SWITZERLAND	45
DENMARK	0

UK HITS WITH ANIMALS IN THEIR TITLES

We're going to show you five songs that have been Top 40 hits in the UK (along with the name of the artist and the year in which they were first hits). In each case there is a word missing which is the name of an animal. We want you to fill in the blank.

_____ ROCK (Elton John, 1972)

RUNNING _____ (Johnny Preston, 1960)

THE _____ SLEEPS TONIGHT (The Tokens, 1961)

EYE OF THE _____ (Survivor, 1982)

UNION OF THE _____ (Duran Duran, 1983)

CROCODILE	48
BEAR	19
LION	84
TIGER	95
SNAKE	11

THE MOONS OF SATURN

According to NASA's official website, there are fifty-three natural satellites (or 'moons') orbiting Saturn which have been discovered and named as of the start of October 2012. We want you to name the most obscure.

We are not including the nine provisional moons yet to be given a name.

AEGAEON	0
AEGIR	0
ALBIORIX	0
ANTHE	0
ATLAS	0
BEBHIONN	0
BERGELMIR	0
BESTLA	0
CALYPSO	1
DAPHNIS	0
DIONE	8
ENCELADUS	3
EPIMETHEUS	0
ERRIAPUS	0
FARBAUTI	0
FENRIR	0
FORNJOT	0
GREIP	0
HATI	0
HELENE	0
HYPERION	1
HYRROKKIN	0
IAPETUS	3
IJIRAQ	0
JANUS	1
JARNSAXA	0
KARI	0
KIVIUQ	0
LOGE	0
METHONE	0
MIMAS	8
MUNDILFARI	0
NARVI	0
PAALIAQ	0
PALLENE	0
PAN	0
PANDORA	1
PHOEBE	0
POLYDEUCES	0
PROMETHEUS	0
RHEA	7
SIARNAQ	0
SKATHI	0
SKOLL	0
SURTUR	0
SUTTUNGR	0
TARQEQ	0
TARVOS	0
TELESTO	0
TETHYS	4
THRYMR	0
TITAN	28
YMIR	0

YOUR *POINTLESS* QUESTIONS ANSWERED

Top tips to win the show

What are your tips for winning *Pointless*?

Well, the obvious answer is: score as low as you can. That is the sure-fire way to *Pointless* glory.

Yes, strangely, I'd got that one.

Ah, very good indeed. Well, there are some quite good *Pointless* tactics that can help, and frankly I'm surprised people don't use them more often.

Such as . . . ?

Blimey, well if you're completely stuck for an answer, try having another go at someone else's wrong answer. They might only have got it a tiny bit wrong ('Cliff Richards', 'Ian Drury' or 'The Tootsie'); you can then wade in with the correct answer ('*Keith* Richards', 'Theatre Royal Drury *Lane*', 'Professor Lord Winston') and clean up. Even if you don't know the correct answer, at least one of the infinite numbers of possible wrong answers has been helpfully ruled out, thus putting you statistically ahead of the game.

Ye-es . . .

Ah, and also see if you can build on answers that have already been given: if Mia on podium two said Beverly Hills Cop for example and scored 17, then go for Beverly Hills Cop II and see how you do – you might even score less. Alright, Mia may never speak to you again but she lives in Barrow-in-Furness for heaven's sake, so what do you care? In Words Rounds always try and think of prefixes that might make your answer more obscure. 'Wrap' will be a high score; 'unwrap' will be less, 'enwrap' still less. I'd probably go for 'bootstrap' in that scenario, which Richard would of course have written down as his prediction of what I'd say at the beginning of the round, so I'd then change it to 'satrap' at the last minute.

Good tip.

Of course 'winning' *Pointless* isn't necessarily about going through to the final, it's about coming on the show and being lovely, and by those criteria nearly everyone who's ever been on *Pointless* has won. Even if they didn't get a trophy and a derisory sum of money to show for it.

DEBUT NOVELS AND THEIR AUTHORS

The following are the debut fiction novels of famous authors. Can you tell us the names of the authors who wrote them?

CATCH-22

FRANKENSTEIN (OR THE MODERN PROMETHEUS)

THE HUNT FOR RED OCTOBER

WHITE TEETH

LORD OF THE FLIES

P.S., I LOVE YOU

THE PICKWICK PAPERS

JOSEPH HELLER 21

MARY WOLLSTONECRAFT SHELLEY 43

TOM CLANCY 9

ZADIE SMITH 11

WILLIAM GOLDING 21

CECELIA AHERN 8

CHARLES DICKENS 59

DEBUT NOVELS AND THEIR AUTHORS

TRAINSPOTTING

TREASURE ISLAND

BRICK LANE

CARRIE

CASINO ROYALE

DIGITAL FORTRESS

THE GREMLINS

IRVINE WELSH	18
ROBERT LOUIS STEVENSON	53
MONICA ALI	6
STEPHEN KING	38
IAN FLEMING	57
DAN BROWN	13
ROALD DAHL	1

WORD ENDING IN 'IND'

Any word that has its own entry in the Oxford Dictionary of English and that ends in the letters 'ind'. We will not allow hyphenated words, trademarks, abbreviations or proper nouns.

If a word shares the same spelling as another word, but is pronounced differently, we are treating them as the same word, and we will only count it as an answer once regardless of how you pronounce it.

BACKWIND	0	REMIND	21
BEHIND	38	RESCIND	15
BIND	72	REWIND	17
BLIND	4	RIND	62
BREAKWIND	0	SIDEWIND	0
CROSSWIND	2	SPELLBIND	0
DOWNWIND	2	SUNBLIND	0
FIND	84	TAILWIND	1
GAVELKIND	0	TAMARIND	4
GRIND	22	UNBIND	1
HEADWIND	0	UNBLIND	0
HIND	69	UNKIND	9
HUMANKIND	1	UNWIND	8
INTERWIND	0	UPWIND	1
KIND	81	WHIRLWIND	1
MANKIND	11	WIND	77
MASTERMIND	0	WOMANKIND	2
MIND	85	WOMENKIND	1
OVERWIND	1	WOODWIND	2
POIND	0	WUNDERKIND	0
PRESCIND	0		
PURBLIND	0		
REBIND	2		

POINTLESS FACT

Sorry Xander . . . (Xander gave the answer 'befriend' and hasn't been allowed to live it down since).

FAMOUS BOXING ENCOUNTERS

We are going to show you five pairs of initials of boxers along with the year and the location where they fought a memorable bout. We would like you to give us the names of both boxers that those initials represent. We're looking for the names of both boxers.

DH VS AH (2010, MANCHESTER)

FB VS LL (1993, CARDIFF)

MA VS JF (1975, MANILA)

MT VS EH (1997, LAS VEGAS)

HC VS CC (1963, LONDON)

DAVID HAYE & AUDLEY HARRISON	0
FRANK BRUNO & LENNOX LEWIS	8
MUHAMMAD ALI & JOE FRAZIER	36
MIKE TYSON AND EVANDER HOLYFIELD	10
HENRY COOPER & CASSIUS CLAY	30

COUNTRIES THAT HAVE HAD A FEMALE LEADER

We are looking for any country which has, or has ever had, a female political leader, prior to the beginning of May 2011.

By 'political leader', we mean president, prime minister or chancellor. We will not accept countries which have had only acting female prime ministers or presidents.

By 'country', we mean any sovereign state, which is or has been a UN member in its own right.

ARGENTINA	6
AUSTRALIA	43
BANGLADESH	2
BRAZIL	7
BULGARIA	0
BURUNDI	0
CANADA	1
CENTRAL AFRICAN REPUBLIC	0
CHILE	0
COSTA RICA	1
CROATIA	1
DOMINICA	0
FINLAND	5
FRANCE	2
GERMANY	34
GUYANA	0
HAITI	0
ICELAND	7
INDIA	20
INDONESIA	1
IRELAND	7
ISRAEL	3
JAMAICA	0
KYRGYZSTAN	1
LATVIA	1
LIBERIA	2
LITHUANIA	2
MACEDONIA	0
MALTA	0
MONGOLIA	1
MOZAMBIQUE	0
NEW ZEALAND	4
NICARAGUA	0
NORWAY	3
PAKISTAN	9
PANAMA	0
PERU	0
PHILIPPINES	0
POLAND	0
PORTUGAL	0
RWANDA	0
SAO TOME AND PRINCIPE	0
SENEGAL	0
SLOVAKIA	2
SOUTH KOREA	0
SRI LANKA	1
SWITZERLAND	2
TRINIDAD AND TOBAGO	0
TURKEY	3
UKRAINE	0
UNITED KINGDOM	48
VENEZUELA	0
YUGOSLAVIA	0

YOUR *POINTLESS* QUESTIONS ANSWERED

The future

How many episodes of *Pointless* have you made?

As of Christmas 2014 we have recorded 821 episodes, which, if you're the person in charge of repeats at the BBC is 1,642 episodes. We have filmed for around 1,143 solid hours, which would be about 47 days straight.

And will it run forever now?

Well nothing lasts forever, except maybe the rail replacement bus service between Royston and Cambridge, but I'm sure we've got a good few years in us yet.

And would you ever leave the show?

So long as Xander stays I would stay. I would miss that big lunk.

And if he left?

I would still stay, and I'd replace him with Sue Barker and maybe a faithful sheepdog.

MAINLAND AFRICAN COUNTRIES WITH A COASTLINE

Any country wholly or partly on the African mainland that has a coastline – that is, any part of its border on any sea or ocean.

Countries must be wholly or partly on the mainland of Africa – we're not looking for island nations.

As always, by country we mean a sovereign state that is a member of the UN, so for example we exclude Western Sahara.

ALGERIA	11	LIBYA	24
ANGOLA	7	MAURITANIA	4
BENIN	2	MOROCCO	37
CAMEROON	1	MOZAMBIQUE	9
DEMOCRATIC REPUBLIC OF THE CONGO	1	NAMIBIA	11
DJIBOUTI	2	NIGERIA	12
EGYPT	36	REPUBLIC OF THE CONGO	5
EQUATORIAL GUINEA	1	SENEGAL	8
ERITREA	3	SIERRA LEONE	5
GABON	3	SOMALIA	19
GHANA	20	SOUTH AFRICA	51
GUINEA	1	SUDAN	13
GUINEA-BISSAU	0	TANZANIA	9
IVORY COAST	19	THE GAMBIA	7
KENYA	35	TOGO	2
LIBERIA	6	TUNISIA	29

ICONIC ALBUM COVERS

We are going to give you clues to twelve iconic album covers, with the name of the singer or band in brackets. We would like you to give us the title of the album.

A baby swims for a dollar (Nirvana)

Public Enemy behind bars (Public Enemy)

A man smoking (Arctic Monkeys)

Two greyhounds (Blur)

Four men seated at a table in the desert (Muse)

Michael Jackson reclining in a white suit (Michael Jackson)

NEVERMIND	21
IT TAKES A NATION OF MILLIONS TO HOLD US BACK	2
WHATEVER PEOPLE SAY I AM, THAT'S WHAT I'M NOT	5
PARKLIFE	13
BLACK HOLES AND REVELATIONS	2
THRILLER	20

...Continued

ICONIC ALBUM COVERS

The original cover featured a working zipper (The Rolling Stones)

Visual representation of the first pulsar discovered (Joy Division)

Paul Simonon smashing his bass on stage (The Clash)

A red cap in the back pocket of a pair of jeans (Bruce Springsteen)

A man dressed as a teddy bear (Kanye West)

A prism divides light (Pink Floyd)

STICKY FINGERS 9

UNKNOWN PLEASURES 4

LONDON CALLING 6

BORN IN THE USA 18

THE COLLEGE DROPOUT 0

THE DARK SIDE OF THE MOON 30

TYPES OF PENGUIN

We are going to show you the names of five species of penguins with the alternate letters of each word removed. We would like you to fill in the gaps for the name of the penguin you think is most obscure.

C _ I _ S _ R _ P

R _ C _ H _ P _ E _

M _ C _ R _ N _

G _ N _ O _

E _ P _ R _ R

CHINSTRAP	**6**
ROCKHOPPER	**14**
MACARONI	**11**
GENTOO	**5**
EMPEROR	**68**

MEMBERS OF ARSENAL'S INVINCIBLES

We would like you to name any Arsenal FC squad member who played or was a named substitute for a Premier League game during the 2003/2004 season. This was the season during which the team did not lose a single English Premier League game, and were dubbed 'The Invincibles'.

ASHLEY COLE	5
DAVID BENTLEY	0
DENNIS BERGKAMP	9
EDU	1
EFSTATHIOS TAVLARIDIS	0
ETAME-MAYER LAUREN	2
FRANCIS JEFFERS	0
FREDRIK LJUNGBERG	6
GAËL CLICHY	0
GILBERTO SILVA	1
GRAHAM STACK	1
JENS LEHMANN	3
JÉRÉMIE ALIADIÈRE	0
JOSÉ ANTONIO REYES	1
JUSTIN HOYTE	0
KOLO TOURÉ	1
MARTIN KEOWN	7
NWANKWO KANU	0
PASCAL CYGAN	1
PATRICK VIEIRA	9
RAMI SHAABAN	0
RAY PARLOUR	3
ROBERT PIRÈS	6
SOL CAMPBELL	5
STUART TAYLOR	0
SYLVAIN WILTORD	1
THIERRY HENRY	24

YOUR POINTLESS QUESTIONS ANSWERED

The *Pointless* Trophy

How big is the *Pointless* Trophy?

Yes of course you'd want to know that because when you see it on the show there's nothing next to it is there? How big do you think it is?

Maybe a foot? How big is it actually?

Well in size, it's not actually that big. It comes in at 120mm tall.

What do you mean *in size*?

Well because in stature it's obviously enormous. Couples who have just knocked their final round into the long grass with three made-up Stranglers singles ('I Love You Baby', 'Missing You Already' and 'It's Pointless!') and watched a possible £8,500 jackpot sail past them, will always say – and in a way that makes me genuinely believe them – that they were only here for the trophy.

What's it made of?

It's a very nice-looking thing, made of glass and weighing in at about 1,083 grams. When we show it to the studio audience, Greg, our floor manager, shines his torch up through it, which always gets a big Ooooooh. You could cut the covetousness with cheese wire.

And do the couples have to share the trophy? Or do they get one each?

No, we give them one each. That would be pretty miserable wouldn't it? Having to share?

Is it true that you can get them on eBay?

Well, they do crop up very occasionally. I could only find two that had been sold. One had fetched £93 and the other £153.87, which I guess isn't bad for a show that's still going. In 2014 a Les Dawson Blankety Blank Chequebook and Pen sold for £280, a Bullseye Tankard for £30 and a Crystal Maze Crystal was unsold at 99p.

CHEMICAL ELEMENTS

We are going to show you a list of criteria. We would like you to give us the name of any chemical element on the periodic table which fulfils at least one of the definitions.

In the case of elements that match more than one condition we will accept the name of the element only once.

As of 1st June 2012, 114 elements have been officially recognized and named by the International Union of Pure and Applied Chemistry (IUPAC).

The criteria are:

Their chemical symbol consists of only one letter

The name of the element has a 'C' in it

The element is a Noble Gas

The name of the element consists of four letters or less

ELEMENT HAS 'C' IN ITS NAME

Element	
Actinium	0
Americium	4
Arsenic	3
Cadmium	4
Caesium	4
Calcium	26
Californium	5
Cerium	1
Chlorine	9
Chromium	4
Cobalt	6
Copernicium	0
Copper	15
Curium	1
Francium	2
Lawrencium	1
Mercury	9
Nickel	1
Protactinium	0
Scandium	0
Silicon	4
Technetium	1
Zirconium	1

ELEMENT HAS 'C' IN ITS NAME / FOUR LETTERS OR FEWER

Element	
Zinc	20

FOUR LETTERS OR FEWER

Element	
Gold	29
Iron	25
Lead	13
Tin	12

NOBLE GAS

Element	
Argon	25
Helium	22
Krypton	1
Radon	4
Xenon	18

NOBLE GAS / FOUR LETTERS OR FEWER

Element	
Neon	31

SINGLE-LETTER SYMBOL

Element	
Boron	8
Fluorine	3
Hydrogen	24
Iodine	4
Nitrogen	14
Oxygen	27
Phosphorus	3
Potassium	16
Sulphur	6
Tungsten	2
Uranium	2
Vanadium	3
Yttrium	0

SINGLE-LETTER SYMBOL / ELEMENT HAS 'C' IN ITS NAME

Element	
Carbon	48

FICTIONAL SETTINGS OF TV SHOWS

The following are all names of fictional places. Which television programme is set in each place?

WALMINGTON-ON-SEA

NEW NEW YORK

BEDROCK

LETHERBRIDGE

ROYSTON VASEY

CRAGGY ISLAND

...Continued

FICTIONAL SETTINGS OF TV SHOWS

CABOT COVE

LANFORD

SUNNYDALE

SUMMER BAY

GREENDALE

WALFORD

MURDER SHE WROTE	**15**
ROSEANNE	**1**
BUFFY THE VAMPIRE SLAYER	**8**
HOME & AWAY	**50**
POSTMAN PAT	**19**
EASTENDERS	**79**

COCKTAILS

We will give you the initial letters of the names of cocktails, and a list of some of the main ingredients typically used to make them according to the International Bartenders Association. What we want you to do is name the cocktail.

PC – WHITE RUM, COCONUT CREAM, PINEAPPLE JUICE

CL – RUM, COLA, LIME

M – RUM, MINT, SUGAR, LIME JUICE

SB – VODKA, CRANBERRY JUICE, GRAPEFRUIT JUICE

KR – CRÈME DE CASSIS, CHAMPAGNE

PINA COLADA	57
CUBA LIBRE	15
MOJITO	20
SEA BREEZE	3
KIR ROYALE	24

SPANISH POP

Any UK Top 40 single released by either Julio Iglesias or Enrique Iglesias or which has them as a featured artist, which reached the Top 40 of the UK chart prior to the beginning of October 2012.

Where a single was a double-A side, we will accept either title.

ADDICTED	0
AMOR	0
BAILAMOS	3
BEGIN THE BEGUINE	6
COULD I HAVE THIS KISS FOREVER	1
DIRTY DANCER	0
DO YOU KNOW? (THE PING PONG SONG)	4
ESCAPE	3
HEARTBEAT	1
HERO	45
HEY!	0
I LIKE IT	4
LOVE TO SEE YOU CRY	0
MAYBE	0
MY LOVE	1
NOT IN LOVE	0
QUIEREME MUCHO	0
TAKIN' BACK MY LOVE	2
TIRED OF BEING SORRY	0
TO ALL THE GIRLS I'VE LOVED BEFORE	4
TO LOVE A WOMAN	0
TONIGHT (I'M LOVIN' YOU)	3

POINTLESS FACT

This was the question, under the name, 'European Pop' which won the largest ever jackpot on the show, £24,750 – with the answer, 'Maybe'.

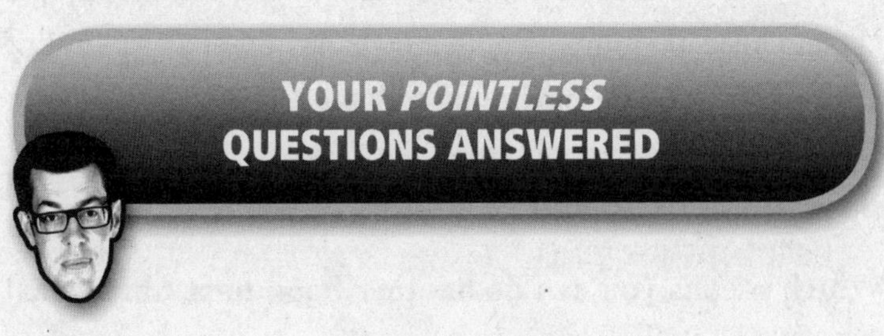

Thank you

Thank you for answering all of my questions!

It's a pleasure! After all, you've been answering mine too.

Yes, and that was also a pleasure, up to the point where my entire family accused me of cheating.

Why did they accuse you of cheating?

Because I'd been cheating.

Oh, ok.

Are there any secrets about *Pointless* that you haven't revealed in this book?

A few, yes. The address where the 200 Club meet up (many of them can't find it, bless them). Which celebrities were told off for conferring. How much Xander drinks. My tattoo. Why we have so many contestants called Dave. Who the Banker is. No, wait, that's a different show. The time Xander killed a guy. Where the *Pointless* trophies are mined. What I write down on my pieces of paper throughout the show. Why the head-to-head podiums look like owls. Whether the plural of 'podium' should be 'podiums' or 'podia'. And, most importantly, what Orville got up to at the *Pointless Celebrities* after-show party.

Which means you can do another book next Christmas!

Bingo. Merry Christmas everyone! Unless, again, you're reading this in paperback, in which case enjoy that choc-ice!

AUSTRALIAN ACTS AND THEIR HITS

We're going to show you the titles of fourteen songs by acts from Australia and New Zealand. Please tell us who had the UK Top 40 hit with each song.

OOH AAH JUST A LITTLE BIT

ROCK AND ROLL DAMNATION

KISS KISS

PUB WITH NO BEER

BORN TO TRY

THE CARNIVAL IS OVER

CAN'T GET YOU OUT OF MY HEAD

GINA G	26
AC/DC	4
HOLLY VALANCE	40
SLIM DUSTY	2
DELTA GOODREM	10
THE SEEKERS	19
KYLIE MINOGUE	70

...Continued

AUSTRALIAN ACTS AND THEIR HITS

TORN

TRULY MADLY DEEPLY

DOWN UNDER

JUMP TO THE BEAT

WEATHER WITH YOU

TOO MANY BROKEN HEARTS

DON'T IT MAKE YOU FEEL GOOD

NATALIE IMBRUGLIA	38
SAVAGE GARDEN	18
MEN AT WORK	20
DANNII MINOGUE	2
CROWDED HOUSE	13
JASON DONOVAN	51
STEFAN DENNIS	6

TYPES OF BREAD

The correct answers in this round will all be types of bread, both leavened and unleavened. The incorrect answers will not be types of bread at all.

BARMBRACK

MELONPAN

RYE

CIABATTA

ELSWICK

FOCACCIA

SOURDOUGH

BARMBRACK	0
MELONPAN	0
RYE	14
CIABATTA	25
ELSWICK	X
FOCACCIA	6
SOURDOUGH	6

...Continued

TYPES OF BREAD

TUGRIK

MARKOUK

BRIOCHE

DAKTYLA

FARRINER

SODA

NAAN

TUGRIK	X
MARKOUK	0
BRIOCHE	4
DAKTYLA	0
FARRINER	X
SODA	26
NAAN	42

ENGLAND FOOTBALLERS NAMED PETER OR PAUL

We are looking for any member of an England World Cup or European Championship squad commonly known by the first name Peter or Paul since 1980, up to the World Cup of 2010. To clarify, we are only looking for players named in the final squad.

WORDS THAT BEGIN WITH A VOWEL AND END WITH '. . . OLOGY'

We are looking for any word that has its own entry in the Oxford Dictionary of English that begins with A, E, I, O or U, and ends with the letters ' . . . ology'. And we will not accept the answer 'ology'.

As ever we will not allow hyphenated words, trademarks or abbreviations, and where a word has two variant spellings, such as a US and a UK spelling, we will accept either, but we will not accept that answer more than once.

acarology	0
aerobiology	0
aerology	1
aetiology	1
agrobiology	0
agrology	0
agrostology	0
algology	0
amphibology	0
anaesthesiology	0
andrology	0
angelology	0
anthology	12
anthropology	15
apology	17
archaeology	23
arcology	0
areology	0
Assyriology	0
astrobiology	0
astrology	20
audiology	7
autecology	0
ecclesiology	0
ecology	22
ecophysiology	0
ecotoxicology	0
Egyptology	4
electrophysiology	0
electrotechnology	0
embryology	0
endocrinology	2
entomology	13
enzymology	0
epidemiology	3
epistemology	1
erotology	0
escapology	8
eschatology	1
ethnoarchaeology	0
ethnology	0
ethnomethodology	0
ethnomusicology	0
ethology	1
etymology	9
exobiology	0
ichthyology	0
iconology	0
ideology	12
immunology	3
Indology	0
iridology	1
oceanology	1
odontology	0
oenology	1
oncology	16
onomasiology	0
ontology	2
oology	0
ophiology	0
ophthalmology	4
orchidology	0
ornithology	24
orthokeratology	0
osteology	0
otolaryngology	0
otology	1
otorhinolaryngology	0
ufology	4
urology	20

Also from

ALEXANDER ARMSTRONG & RICHARD OSMAN

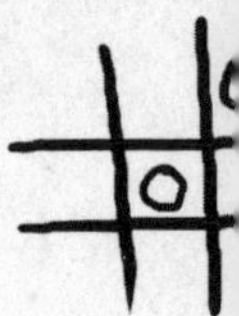